James Hawker's Journal

A VICTORIAN POACHER

D0273051

In Memory of

JOHN TUDOR WALTERS

for whom this book was written

CONTENTS

	Introduction	ix
	Acknowledgements	xxiii
I	My Earliest Recolections	I
II	I Land in Oadby and Become a Poacher	II
III	Politics and Bicycling	21
IV	Some Narrow Shaves	30
V	Another Near Thing	42
VI	In The Season of the Year	47
VII	Encounters With Animals	54
VIII	Calling the Hare	64
IX	Looking Back	68
X	Portrait of Oadby	81
XI	Village Concert	96
XII	If They Only Knew	99
XIII	Every Man A Poacher	104
XIV	Foxes, Ferretts and Courting Couples	109

INTRODUCTION

Few men without any schooling have written a book. Few poachers, fired with fierce bitterness against the land-owning gentry, have enjoyed the friendship of country squires. These two facts alone mark James Hawker as a man of rare character.

Hardly less surprising, this life-long poacher who at an early age mastered the language of the woods and fields where a squawking blackbird, a spoor in the mud, or a piece of dung may reveal so much, found himself the victim of a perennial conflict between the rural pursuits in which he delighted and that passionate concern with social justice and politics which absorbed so much of his time. He was a poacher—and something of a local politician—because hard times had made him so; and those who knew him well noticed that the energy which flowed from his sturdy frame seemed to be kindled and released as much by political campaigns fought on behalf of Charles Bradlaugh as by the excitements of a starry night when he would tread the coverts and the hedgerows matching his wits against those of the wild creatures and their protectors—the gamekeepers and county police.

How this volume comes to be published forms a strange story. Stirred by the weird, sustained churring of the nightjars on Chailey Common, Sussex, where they repeatedly used the roofs of two cottages as song-posts, I wrote an article about them for *Country Life*. My sister promptly reported that her husband's brother-in-law, John Tudor Walters, whom I had never met, had nightjars nesting around his garden laid out by the sculptor Sir William Reid Dick, in the heart of the West Sussex woods at Fittleworth, near Wisborough Green. Would I care to visit him?

I shall never forget the experience. First Mr. Tudor Walters, a retired surveyor whose youth had been spent in Leicestershire, introduced me to the well-wooded garden where nightjars emerged at dusk, fluttering across the lawns beside the house and perching slantwise on the boughs of oak and silver birch, clapping their wings and uttering loud bubbling cries as birds of the opposite sex flew near.

Then, with somewhat mixed feelings, I saw my host's massive Edwardian hoard of birds' eggs, carefully boxed and labelled and firmly fixed to every door. I admired his fine collection of Georgian clocks that made the very air vibrate as they boomed and chimed each hour. Finally, I was shown his library.

Introduction

We handled an old edition of Gilbert White and the familiar works of the Victorian naturalists. And then seizing a dark, stiff-bound volume that looked like a Bible, he said: 'You might care to see this book written in his own hand by an old friend of mine. He presented it to me before we left our home at Oadby in Leicestershire.'

Pasted on the inside of the front cover was a press photograph of Count Leo Tolstoy and his wife. There followed a list of the contents and then a photograph of a young actress, Gladys Cooper, with her child. Amid a number of press cuttings fixed to the end of the volume I noticed photographs of Charles Bradlaugh, Keir Hardie, Mr. Gladstone, Tom Sayers, the boxer, and Augustine Birrell; and one page bearing the date 1899 was devoted to a description and picture of a spring-gun designed for use against poachers. Curious, I began to read the manuscript in a neat sloping hand headed *The Life of a Poacher*.

'Born in the year 1836 in Daventry Northamptonshire of very Poor Parents my Father was a Tailor by Trade my Mother Assisted him at his work times were very Bad and they found it Hard to Live.'

I paused and enquired who the author might be. It was then that I heard for the first time of James Hawker, a skilful poacher whose friends found him as kindly as he was amusing and stimulating. Year after year, my host explained, Hawker had poached pheasants, hares, and rabbits from the woods and fields of his father, Sir John Tudor Walters. Yet such was the personal charm and keen intelligence of the old poacher that eventually he was elected a member of the Oadby School Board.

It was a surprising appointment, for Hawker's politics were far removed from those of the local gentry who largely governed the neighbourhood. Even his enemies, however, acknowledged that Hawker was an honest rogue, a man who had taken to poaching because of hunger, and who maintained the habit to the end of his days because it absorbed and thrilled his whole being. Once a man has grown adept at using a gun and a gate-net in the not so silent hours of the night, it becomes hard for him to lie in bed when the wind is just strong enough to make the Scots pines sound like the sea, and there is barely light for a fox to observe the prey it has caught by scent and sound, or the gamekeeper to see the rabbits that come bounding out of the blackness into the poacher's long net.

Hawker worked hard for his village. Men who liked neither his poaching nor his politics, and who would cheerfully have seen him locked up for seizing their pheasants, did not hesitate to pause and converse with him of country matters when they met him in the lanes. They admired the way he had reared three orphaned children, one of them a cripple, and the manner in which he helped with the village concerts, visited his sick friends, and served on a number of parochial committees. They relished, too, that spirit of independence that prompted him to speak as an equal with squire and stockman alike. None troubled to question his belief that the poor man at his gate was just as important in the sight of God as the rich man in his castle.

Despite a certain underlying impatience and bitterness produced by his experiences as a poverty-stricken youth, Hawker proved a useful committee-man, with a rich store of commonsense. The men of wealth and influence on the Oadby School Board for the most part found their opinion of the poacher steadily rising. Thus Sir John Tudor Walters was not unduly dismayed when Hawker gained the friendship of his son.

The pair would talk for hours of the wild life of woodland and meadow, Hawker recounting his experiences as a poacher in two or three Midland counties, and the boy telling of his adventures when out shooting and egg-collecting. Their friendship deepened when, early in the present century, the poacher presented the young naturalist with the volume that is printed here.

It was one of three books which Hawker wrote

with his thick pen and thin ink, though what happened to the other volumes and how much they differed from this one, it is impossible to say.

Thanks to the kindness of several Oadby residents, and particularly of Mr. K. Meakin, an old friend of Hawker who has been to considerable trouble to help me, it has been possible to expand somewhat the intimate impressions of the poacher which the late John Tudor Walters first planted in my mind. Broadly built and wiry, which made him appear a little short of stature—though he was, in fact, five feet eight inches in height—and with a fringe of grey beard, Hawker is best remembered by some of his friends for the brightness of his eyes. There was a good brain, people felt, behind that alert expression; and the Sunday School teacher who spent his spare time teaching the poor boy to read and write must have found him an eager and responsive pupil.

Indeed, my first reaction on reading his manuscript, which Tudor Walters suggested might form the subject of an article for *The Countryman,* was one of astonishment that a man who knew so little of the rules of English grammar, and less of the principles of punctuation, should write with such admirable simplicity and vigour. And in a day when men often wrote long sentences James Hawker knew the value of the short one.

Here, I felt, was something too good to waste on one article. Would not *The Countryman* care to print, say, a third of it? The Editor, Mr. John Cripps, was quick to appreciate its value and in due course portions of this book appeared in his columns, though not always in the order given here. It was these extracts which aroused the interest of the Oxford University Press.

I have tried to edit the work as little as possible, leaving uncorrected Hawker's surprisingly few spelling errors and the mis-use of capitals. Some of the chapter headings are mine, and a considerable amount of material has been re-arranged to prevent repetition; but it has seldom been necessary to adjust Hawker's sentences or to insert phrases that are not his.

Meeting a writer face to face can be a disillusioning experience. But those who knew Hawker in the flesh seem to have found him as lively as his memoirs. Invariably they discovered him wearing a long covert coat that came down over his legs and which contained numbers of secret pockets where hares and pheasants could be hidden. He usually walked with a slight limp, not through any physical handicap but because a sawn-off rifle was normally carried down his trouser leg.

It was the desperate need for food for himself and his family which first prompted him to poach, as many a Leicestershire audience used to learn at election time. For it was the habit of the local Asquith Liberals to invite the poacher on to their platform to talk of his experiences in the 'hungry forties' when he had laboured in the fields as a 'crow-starver' or stone-picker at a wage of a shilling a week.

Soon the boy made a habit of setting snares for rabbits and hares and knocking down pheasants from their roosts. For even when his own family had enough food, there were neighbours who had not.

Once poaching gets into the blood, it is hard to expel. Hawker might stay indoors in a hard frost when a poacher's footsteps could sound through the silent air to the ears of rabbits and hares hundreds of yards away; but he was often out with the long net as the skies darkened and the wind stirred without beating down the leaves and twigs from the trees. On moonlight nights he learned to walk the woods and copses, never treading far from cover and always keeping within the shadows.

His skill in knowing where to look for the partridge and the hare and how to train a ferret—though he never seems to have troubled himself with a dog—was backed by mounting bitterness against the landowners who employed armed keepers to police the woods and copses which God had made for all. For there was a deep religious strain in Hawker, a sacramental sense of the sanctity of all creation, so that like John Ray and the seventeenth century naturalists, he saw the intricate nest of the chaffinch and the innate solicitude of hen pheasants for their young as proof of the wonder and majesty of God.

It was not the divine will that children cried with hunger; it was the fault of the 'system' that had thrown up a ruling class who fed their pheasants on the best hard-boiled eggs while working-class housewives faced empty cupboards. Stirred with a sense of compassion for his neighbours and a deepening hatred for their oppressors, he would go out into the darkness, unaware perhaps of how much the beliefs which shaped his conduct owed to the teaching of Christ and Karl Marx and the example of Robin Hood.

And the habit stuck. Times might change, fortunes alter. Rather than face unemployment Hawker, who was a skilled cobbler, willingly worked in a hosiery factory, a leather works, as a groom and as a farmworker. And all the time he poached— except when politics or journeys on his bicycle absorbed so much of his time that he simply could not manage it.

Always he came back to poaching in the end.

Again and again he wrote: 'If I am able, I will poach till I die.' And he did.

It is fortunate that he possessed a retentive memory or this book might never have been written. For he does not seem to have kept a notebook—a misfortune for the student of wild life. Nor was he always sound when interpreting the behaviour of birds and mammals. In believing that it is the song of the skylarks which 'tells' the hares when it is dawn, he overlooked how sensitive most wild creatures are to changes of light; and while we know far too little about the influence of rabbits and hares on each other, there is not much evidence that hares cannot abide 'the smell of rabbetts'.

Few men, however, could equal his skill in capturing live hares. A witness has described to me how his brother watched Hawker silently walk to a field gate and call the hares, whereupon the animals raised their ears for a second. Then Hawker sauntered across the field in the general direction of one hare, though taking care not to look it in the eye. The hare seemed undecided whether to leap away or remain; in the end it waited. Hawker quietly edged nearer. Then throwing himself down he caught the animal as other men might snatch a rabbit.

His study of wild life was no form of escapism but rather, in James Fisher's phrase, an escape into reality. He was a good mixer, quick to interest men with his tales of birds and mammals, and young people, particularly, seemed to relish his dry sense of humour. Thus when Mr. K. Meakin, as a boy of fourteen, chanced to meet him one day on the borders of Sir Arthur Hazlerigg's estate at Noseley Hall, the pair fell into conversation and the poacher asked 'Young master, do you want to see something funny?'

Hawker led him through a field and into the woods at the back of the Hall. For a moment, admits Mr. Meakin, the boy was inclined to hesitate, for these woods were guarded like the Bank of England. 'We're all right,' said Hawker. 'Sir Arthur, all the keepers, and most of the farm men have gone to a big shoot away over there, and it's all quiet down here.'

'He led me,' writes Mr. Meakin, 'to a rick in the woods, and on a ride there were a score of pheasants staggering about in an advanced state of inebriation. Hawker had fed them well on raisins soaked in rum or gin.'

As the birds pecked at their food, often failing by several inches to connect, Hawker wandered among them, picking up a number and feeling which were the fattest. These had their necks wrung and were quickly thrust down his trouser legs. Then as the pair returned to the road, Hawker said sternly:

'Now, young master, you see what drink does to you.'

The poacher was not always in so calm and cheerful a mood. There was a notorious occasion at a village meeting when he clashed over some local matter with the late Alfred Turner, of Brox Hill, Oadby, a well known hosiery manufacturer and farmer. Hawker embarrassed his fellows by heatedly describing Turner to his face as 'a hard-fisted old Tory.' Turner responded by saying: 'If ever you come on my land again, I'll have you arrested for the poaching blackguard you are.'

They did not speak again for a year or more. Then one night in a thick fog, they happened to meet stepping off a tram. Turner spoke first. 'Jim,' he said, 'I think we were both fools at that meeting. Will you shake hands and be friends?'

The old poacher clutched his hand. 'Thank God, Mr. Turner. Sir, this has kept me awake at night. I'm glad we can be friends again.' Slowly the couple trudged along the village street, talking amicably together. As they parted, Turner said: 'I'm pleased we're friends again. If ever you want a rabbit, I'll tell my men you can come and get it on my land any time you like.'

'Thank you kindly, Mr. Turner,' replied Hawker, 'but I'm sorry you've said that. You've been honest with me, so I'll be quite frank with you. I shan't get any more of your rabbits than I've been poaching from you over this past year—only now you've given me permission it won't be half as much fun getting them.'*

In fact, several landowners, Sir John Tudor Walters among them, found that the best way to stop Hawker poaching on their land was to grant him permission to do so.

He remained fit and active to the end of his days, and when about sixty-five years old entered a race for the over-fifties at the Oadby village sports. Spectators at that event report that he 'won by over half the distance.'

Within a few months of his death in 1921, it was not unusual for residents to hear the crack of his rifle around sunrise. An hour or so later, as the village came to life, people would ask their neighbours 'Did you hear Mister Hawker getting himself some dinner?'

Yet he would have been appalled by the cruelties and craftiness of so many modern poachers— mechanised bandits who slaughter deer and game-birds not in order to eat nor for the fun of it, but because it is safer than burgling a bank. Hawker, no doubt, could be ruthless when cornered; but he was no criminal, only an adventurous countryman with his own moral code, a villager who was trodden on

---

* This incident was often described by Mr. Turner before his death.

but never broken, oppressed by gentlemen who were extremely kind, preyed on by police who delighted to poach when off duty.

As we have seen, he hated 'the Class', yet counted a number of close friends among them. He deplored the failure of his fellow workers to unite for social justice, yet he never lost his faith in them. He thanked God for the fine example of pheasants tending their young; then he shot them. He moved about the Midlands a good deal to evade the police; yet he was never a nomad. He grew strong roots and gloried in the fact. 'Dear old Oadby stands second to none spiritually, intellectually and politically. Indeed, it takes the cake politically.'

We can hardly call him typical of the Victorian villager. Yet he must have been one of many in every age who were rough spoken but rich in humour, sturdy and independent, quick to mistrust much of what they hear and some of what they see, half Christian and half pre-Christian. When Hawker died nearly forty years ago, at the age of 84, and they buried him in Oadby Cemetery, a friend was heard to say 'There was never any real 'arm in 'im.' And to-day in the parish of Oadby, which has changed so much since the poacher's day, there are still one or two people who remember James Hawker. 'He was a proper character,' they say.

ACKNOWLEDGEMENTS

While much of this book has not previously been published, long passages from certain chapters first appeared in *The Countryman*. I am grateful to the Editor of that publication for kindly granting permission for these sections to be reproduced here. I am also indebted to him for much help and advice when preparing the manuscript for publication. My thanks are due also to Ann Sangiovanni (*née* Tudor Walters) of Rome; to the Churchwardens of Oadby Parish Church, Mr. Denis W. Marriott, Chief Financial Officer of the Oadby Urban District Council, and the Librarian of Northampton Central Public Library who went to much trouble to help me; and, above all, much is owed to the aid I have received from Mr. K. Meakin and other old friends of James Hawker, and to Mr. W. D. Allen, of Shearsby, who kindly loaned the artist some interesting prints of the old Oadby which the poacher knew and liked so well. The cottage beside the church, shown on page 81, was the home of James Hawker.

I

MY EARLIEST RECOLECTIONS

I was born in 1836 in Daventry, Northamptonshire, of very Poor Parents. My Father was a Tailor by Trade and my Mother assisted him in this work. Times were very Bad and they found it hard to Live. At the age of six I remember my Father working in a Garrett where I Slept, until ten o'clock at night. At the age of eight I went to work in the Fields, scaring Birds for seven days a week at a wage of one shilling. This sum Bought my Mother a four Pound Loaf.

At the age of twelve I went to work at a Boot

Shop. At the first Shop where I worked sat two Old Men who had Fought in the Battle of Waterloo in 1815. They were making Army Boots. When they took there work to the Shop, they was paid no Booking money like it is today. I often thought this was a great inducement for men to Drink—as the Shoe-Maker often Does. Most manufacturers kept a Provision Shop and the Man who Spent the most of his wage had the Most and Best work. The same Spirit Lives to Day. This was called the Truck Shop. Parliament swept it away.

The mid-1840's were wretched times. Sheep Stealing, Highway Robbery and Burglary were common. It was not Safe to go out after Dark. If a Man stole a Sheep he Had 14 years Transportation. If hunger made a man go into the woods to get a pheasant, he too would get fourteen years. Two men in Oadby Had 14 years—Jack Baurn, Bill Devonport—for attempting to take Pheasants in Tugley Wood, in 1847, so this is No Dream.

In 1845, John Bright and Richard Cobden was Speaking in all the Large Centres of Industry in England, in favour of the Repeal of the Corn Laws. At Last after almost every Prison was Filled with Bread Rioters the Tory Party gave way. I Have se Sir Robert Peel's Effigy Carried through the Streets and Burnt in the Market Place. Soldiers were Brought from Weedon Barracks to Clear the Streets at the Point of the Baynott. In 1846 Peel Repealed the Corn Laws.

At the age of 12, My Father Took a Shop at a Rent of 8 shillings Per Week in the Hopes of Bettering our Condition by Dealing in new and Second Hand Clothes. In two years we Had the Busy* for the Rent, but they was very Humane and we took most of our Furniture.

We went to Live in a very Poor Part of the Town. In this year 1850—when I was 14 years of age—I first commenced to Poach. My Father Had Tried to Better our Position Lawfully and had failed. So I was determined to try some other means. I was surrounded by every Temptation. The Class that starved me certainly tempted me with all their Game and Fish. Having no Gun, no net, no Dog, I was content for a time to Poach Fish with a Ball of String Hooks and Small Baits. I would catch Pike Ranging from one to ten Pounds each.

At this time—1852—men were encouraged to join the Militia. Lord Panmure Brought in a Bill promising that any Man who joined up before the 12th May, 1854, should not be kept out for more than 56 Days in any one year. Thousands of men joined, receiving 10 shillings when they were in. During 1853 me and two Companions went and joined. I said I was 18, so you se I told a Lie for I was only

* Bailiff.

[3]

17. I Did not join to Serve the Queen. I wanted the ten shillings to by a Gun and when I got it I Bought one.

Unfortunately it was of Little use when I got it, and I had to wait till I got more money before buying a good one. It was a Flint and Steel weapon and had no Gun Cap and if the Day or Night was Damp the Priming—that is the Powder—would be Like Putty and it would not explode. Many a time I Have Pulled the Trigger at a Pheasant and I Have Had to Leave him Sitting in his Glory as the Gun wouldn't go off!

My two Pals Spent there money in Drink. They are both Dead now through that. One Died in a Lunatic Asylum. Many a time I Have Begged of them to Let the Drink alone and come and roam the Beautiful Fields with me. Sometimes in the Small Hours of the morning when coming Home with a Hare or Pheasant I have peept into a Pub and seen these two sitting fast asleep. Drink Pubs did not Close in those Days as they do now.

Before long the Militia was called up for Training. When Disbanded I received £1. Then I bought a Percussion—that means a Gun Cap—and then I Done Better. No man in the world was more Happy than me. I had a weapon I could Depend on. If men only knew today the weapon they possess Politicaly,

How Happy Millions of us might be if they only knew how to use it.

In 1854 the Militia was Called up for Garison Duty. I was sent with the Northamptonshire Regiment to Dublin. I was there during the Crimean War. I made the most of it by not Drinking. I Had wondered many times why we took our Rifles and 20 Rounds of Ball Cartridges to Church. I Don't wonder now. We could not Trust the People. There is Something Rotten in the State when we Can't Do that. A Kinder Hearted Race of People never Lived. I mounted Guard Several times at a Prison called Mount Joy. It should Have been called Misery. It was full of Political Prisoners. I was Full Corporal and I had a Chance sometimes to Slip a Bit of Tobacco into the Hands of these Soldiers. Don't Forget these Poor Creatures.

While in Dublin I was Paid a Compliment from a temperance Point of view. I was Selected by the Sergeant Major to take a Deserter to Bury in Lancashire. He said I was 'Proof against Getting Drunk.'

One evening—October 25—after reading the Charge of the Light Brigade, I was playing my Concertina and the Men were Dancing when Captain Vivian came to the Door.

'Corporal Hawker,' he shouted. 'Where did you Get that Thing?'

'I bought it, Sir,' I told him.

'Surely not out of your pay?' he said.

'Yes, sir,' I replied. 'I bought it to keep the men out of the Canteen. It cost me ten shillings.'

He put five shillings in my Hand, a reward for setting the Men a Good Example.

During March, 1855, it came to the knowledge of Some of the Men that Lord Panmure's Act of that year—the Army Services Amendment Act—provided for the calling up of men for periods of two or three years. (Lord Panmure expressed his readiness to recruit long-service men by compulsion if necessary).

The men Lay Down there Arms in the Barrack Square and refused to Drill. Lord Burleigh Begged of the men to take up there arms, saying 'This is Mutiny'.

At 9.30 p.m. the bugle Sounded again and the Orderly Sergeant announced the Order sending Home all Men who enlisted under the Act.

When I had to appear at Leicester for Militia Training, my wife and Family would come with me for the month. When training was done and I was about to Depart, the Police would try and capture me for I still owed £8-0-0 for killing Hares. I had to be a little foxey at these times.

The adjutant, Captain Grimston, would not give

me up till training was over. Then I had to Look Out for Myself. One morning at Staff Parade I saw a Revenue Officer talking to Captain Grimston. (I was a Sergeant at the time, a rank I kept for 17 years). He called me out of the Ranks and asked me what I intended to Do Respecting the £8-0-0.

'I'll give you two pounds out of my own Pocket and go Round among the other officers and get you the Rest if you will promise never to Poach again,' he said.

I thanked him for his kind offer, but added that if he offered £100 I could not make such a promise. 'If you Promise they won't capture me before we Break up,' I said, 'I'll see that they don't afterwards.'

This gentleman afterwards became the Chief Constable of Leicestershire County Police. He committed suicide by blowing out his brains. The last word the man ever spoke to me was when I left the Regiment. 'If ever you want a Reccomendation for anything,' he said, 'it will do you good to write to me.'

To show you how many had been Dished prior to this, Notices had been put up that any man who will volunteer for Gibraltar Shall have £2.11 and a week's pass. 600 men volunteered. They were sent to Plymouth. Men who had enlisted after May 12th,

1854 and not volunteered was sent to Northampton to form a Depot.

After I had been home for a few weeks doing a bit of poaching and a bit of work, Notice was sent all over the County that any 56 Day man Can take his Discharge if he will Re-engage, and have another 10/-. I was always Ready to get a Bob or two Easy, so I made up My mind to take my Discharge and Re-engage. The Regiment was now Disbanded and instead of the Sergeant first Discharging me as a 56 Day man, he took me on as a new recruit. Don't laugh but I was in the Army Double when the Regiment was Called up in 1856. I received two summonses as a 56 Day man and a new recruit. I went to my Company as a 56 day man and when the Roll was called: 'James Hawker, Recruit, No Reply' I Could Not Help Laughing. But I kept Dark about It.

We 56 Day men were soon sent home again and when I had been there for a few weeks, the Daventry Police Came to enquire How it was I had been out and Done my Training and yet was a new recruit and a Deserter?

This was no case of mistaken identity, they said, for all the facts were accurate—height five feet, eight inches; Dark hair; Dark eyes. Who could help but laugh at all this. At last they took me to the Depot. But they would not have me there for they knew I had been up and Done my Training. So the Police took me to the Northampton Prison saying:– 'We have done our Duty. We will now send to the Regiment and tell them where you are and they can Do What they Like.'

I lay in Northampton Prison for a month before the Escort came for me. It was a Saturday afternoon when they burst into my cell and let me out into the streets to the station. One of the escort was carrying a Brown Parcel containing a Pork Pie from a Dear Old Mother to her Dear Boy at Plymouth. When we arrived at Bath there was a wait of two hours and the escort told me to look after their rifles while they went off into the town; if they were not back in an hour I could eat the Pie. I did not wait but started at once on the Pork Pie. In an hour and a half I had finished the pie and there was no sign of the Escort. So I went out into the town and looked for them. I found them arm in arm and dead Drunk. It was with difficulty that I persuaded the Station Master to let them continue on the journey as my Escort. Then after riding all night they pulled themselves to-gether and Put me in the charge of the Guard.

After a short stay in the Guard Room Cell I was handed over to the Civil Powers. In fact, they did not know what to do with me or what Charge to Prefer. I was Brought before the Magistrate at Plymouth and strange to say, the Chairman was

Colonel Hawker. This was the first time I met a man outside my family with our own name. My name, I think, Played a very Important Part in securing my release.

The Magistrate began by asking, 'What have you against this man? You charge him with desertion. He has been up and Done his Training, Has served nearly 12 months in Dublin, has a Good Character, never been in dificulties or in the Defaulters' Book. What does this mean? Surely something is wrong. Now my man, if you can assist us and it should incriminate you in any way I will take that into Consideration.'

After these kind words I Let The Cat Out of the Bag. 'Sir, I would have done this before,' I told him, 'But I did not want to get into Trouble the man who made a mistake over me. The Sergeant took me on without first Discharging me.' The Chairman said, 'This enlistment falls to the ground. Send the man home.'

I was marched to the station and received a ticket for home. Thus endeth the first chapter in my military life.

II

I LAND IN OADBY AND BECOME
A POACHER

Home once more I Had not been there long before I Had the first Lesson in Politics—though
not my Last. Having no Schooling—my writing and
spelling Proves this—I could understand and as I
grew older I became almost a Republican. But we
must wait till we can Convince the People before we
Reach that Gaol.

In 1857 an Election was Pending between Lord
Althorpe the present Earl Spencer and a man of the
name Fikey. There were only two parties—Tory and

Liberal. No Unionists took part in that election. Today there are three parties but only two Policys. When I find three Partys in a State, it reminds me of two men wearing one coat and saying they feel comfortable. Unionism is Double-Dyed Toryism for they are Wolves in Sheep's clothing. The Richest Man stood the best chance at this election. It was not Brains but Gold that Ruled in those days. Pubs was thrown open to the People and Plenty of Drink provided, though the working Man Had no Vote then. Polling was eight o'clock till four. When it was a Close Run I have seen Captain Watkins of Daventry Hold up a Ten Pound Note for a Tory vote. We knew every hour How Each Party Stood. They would Engage all the Roughs as Special Constables, not to Keep the Peace but because they might break it. I was one several times. We was marched into the National School and Kept there till the Election was over. There was plenty of Eating and Drinking and five Shillings each. They knew if we was at Liberty what Part we Should Play. For it was our Natural Instinct to Look upon the Tory as our Greatest Enemy.

I don't think today—after a Lapse of sixty years —much of what some men think and say. Today we have the Vote. Some are Entering Parliament. Curse yourselves, it is ourselves who Make Parliaments.

It is true some of the Noblest Minded men in

England are Tories. But when we send them to Westminster we are Placing Square Pegs in Round Holes. There's too much of Follow My Leader about the Tory Party. When will the Working Men Send their Own Class to Rule? The Tories are only doing what we Refuse to Do—which is Watch Our Own Interests.

Towards the end of the year 1857 when the Leaf Began to Fall, we thought there might be a few Pheasants at Roost. So at about 8.30 p.m. one night, a Jap named Tom Came to the Door.

'Are you ready, Jim?' said he.

'Yes,' I replied. 'You go on and I'll catch you later on.'

We had a mile to walk to Reach the Wood and I put my Gun in my Pockit and Followed soon afterwards. When I caught him he was Leaning over a Gate the worse for Drink.

'If I'd known you was in Drink, I wouldn't have Come,' I said.

'Jimmy, Don't Tinker,' he said. 'I'll be alright before we get there.'

To Reach the wood we had to Cross the Park in Front of Badley House. When we got well inside the Park Gates out flew the Keepers.

Like me, Tom was a Good Runner when Sober, but this time Drink began to tell its tale after he had covered 200 yards. He rolled like a Ship in a Storm. Suddenly Down he went and the Head Keeper was soon on Top of Him.

Tom shouted: 'Jim, come back—there's only two of 'em.'

I went back and found they were Father and Son, Simon Braunston and Sam Braunston. When I look at that Picture in my seventieth year, I often think it would be worthy of a Painter's brush. My Pal Had the man under him and was tossing him about like a Cat with a Mouse. He was a very powerful Lad and Drink for a time added to his strength. As the old gamekeeper lay on his Back with the Moon Shining on his Face, it was a picture I Shall Never Forget.

The son, Sam, was carrying a Double-Barrelled Gun and Has I stood there he put it to his shoulder Fully Cocked, saying: 'If you come another yard I'll let Daylight into you.'

The Father cried: 'Put that Gun Down, Sam. Jim, you go away. Don't make bad worse. We shan't loose Tom and when we've Locked him up we'll come and Fetch you.'

I went away. Had there been no Gun in this Social Drama, things might have been Different.

They remanded Tom in the hopes of Getting Me. They gave him Bail. He soon went and enlisted in the Artillery and I Have never seen that Lad since.

I ran home as quick as I Could and Drew my
Travelling Card. For by this time I was a Trade
unionist—almost before I knew what it Meant. But
I knew even then Has I know now that in the
Union is Strength. I Belonged to the Card-Weavers'
Association.

Soon I had made my way to Northampton and on
Sunday morning set off for Leicester.

When I reached the Little Village I am living in
today—1904—it was about four o'clock in the afternoon. I heard Singing in the Little Wesleyan Chapel
in the village street. I stopped where two young
women were standing listening to the singing. My
thoughts wandered Back to my Home for I knew at
that time that My Mother would be in Chapel and
She Would be wondering where I was. I caused my
Mother a Lot of Trouble, but I made it up in other
ways. If there is a Rough in a Family, he is Generaly
the Mother's first care.

Had my surroundings been different—like those
of the young men of today—I might never have
Been a Poacher. So much for the Dark Days of
Protection.

My thoughts were interrupted when one of the
young women said to the Other: 'Sarah, see how
that Chap is Staring at you.'

Little Did I think that those words Spoken in jest
would Someday Prove true.

After the Singing I made my way towards Leicester. As I reached Stoughton Lane there were so many nicely Dressed people on the Road that I felt ashamed and hid myself till dusk. When I reached our Club House, the Prince Regent kept by Jimmy Johnson, I received one and sixpence and a Bed. Had I not been a union man, I might have been compelled to Beg or Steal. After taking a Little Food I was soon in Bed for the Pub had no Charm for me.

On Monday I got work and good Lodgings and Remained in Leicester until the Spring. Then I thought I would Have a Ramble. I joined the Leicester Militia under the name of James Collis. I was known by no other name and am Called by it today by many men. I received ten shillings.

Then I tired of Leicester and set off for Coventry, for I did not really care where I went. A young man with Ribbons flying fell in with me and asked me if I would take the Shilling and enlist. I did so and was soon sent with others to Aldershot North Camp. H. still lives but I don't intend to mention his name. Let not thy Right Hand know what Thy Left Hand Doeth.

The Aldershot Camp was my home until July, 1858. During my stay there I proved beyond all Doubt that I Could never be trained to Kill Peasants, but Pheasants were another matter. I knew that the Class what trained me to shoot Peasants would kill

me or at least imprison me for Killing what God
sent for everyman—the pheasants.

So I made up my mind to Desert. Once more I
longed to Ramble through the Beautiful Fields. I
told my comrade of my intention. Almost all soldiers
have a Comrade who is trusted with our Little
Secrets. But I said not a word to anyone else.

He asked me how I could get away with so many
Military Police surrounding the camp. But where
there's a will there's a way. When the next Batch of
Recruits came in, I Slipt into one of their suits of
Clothes. I did not have far to go to the camp
boundry. I knew that once passed the pub called the
Tumble Down Dick I should be safe.

A Big Gun was always fired at half past nine in
the evening and again at ten o'clock Last Post. If
you are found out after that without a pass you are
taken prisoner. Even a civilian passing through the
camp may be suspected and detained. When the
First Gun Fired my Comrade walked a Short Distance with me, Shook Hands and Bid me Good
Night and Good Luck. In a short time when near
the Boundry the Second Gun Fired. That meant the
police were having a Tussle with men without
passes. I slipped past them and walked eight miles
without meeting a soul.

Soon I wanted to sleep and seeing a waggon
Loaded with Pea Sticks Standing by the Side of a

Wood, I climbed on top where no one was likely to find me. I slept till the Sun's warmth woke me. Then I set off for Reading. But not before I stood for a few minutes watching four Women Reaping in a very novel way. Each had a Broom Handle. They would Push it into the corn and then pull it towards them. Then the lengths of corn were gathered up and tied. One young woman said: 'Lad, do you Want a Drink? It won't hurt yer.' I thanked her and she gave me a Horn of Sider.

When I reached Reading—with a Little Money in my pocket—I decided to take the train for Southam. Unfortunately I got into the wrong train which took me to Leamington. I had not enough money to pay the extra Fare. But I told the Station Master that I had a Sister Living outside Leamington Station. If he would send a Porter with me, she would pay. He was glad to get me out of his hands and sent me off with the Porter.

The moment we got outside, I Ran Away. The Porter just Stood and Laughed. It was the Best Thing he Could Do. I then made my own way to Leicester. I Had a Long Day's March, walking till 9.30. Then I sat down near the Side of a Large Spinney near Nuneaton. It was a lovely evening, Everywhere as Still as Death.

As I sat there I was comparing the Past and the Present. What I had left was so noisy. Where I sat was so quiet. Soon I fell asleep. I wakened to hear a Beautiful Pheasant. This was good game country.

A gamekeeper came by on his round and to Kill time he sat down and Had a Smoke and a Chat. Then off I went again towards Leicester which I Reached before Dinner time. I went to my Old Lodgings in Town Hall Lane and Most of the afternoon was spent in Chat. They would want to know what I Did not intend to tell them.

To encourage me to give up Roaming, my Landlady, Mrs. Reeves, said: 'If you will Stop and get down to your Work, I'll get you a new suit of Clothes. Pay me how you can.' As I Had not had a Good suit in my Life—only what the Military provided—I accepted her offer. In a few weeks I found myself in Oadby dressed to Death. I did not go there in search of the Girl I saw near the Chapel. She had never Crossed my Mind again. No, the attraction which brought me there was Game. Often it was Game what Drove me from my Home.

When I returned home I asked my Landlord if He would go and Live there. He was quite willing but he owed a little Back Rent. We paid that and on October 6th, 1858, we Landed safely in our New Home.

I soon made many friends and the more I know of this village, the Better I Like it. The first morning I looked out of my Bedroom Window into the fields near White Horse pub. I saw two hares in Gun

Shot. I sent a note to my Mother: 'Send my gun. Don't forget the name's Collis.' That was the name I was married in. For two years my wife knew me by no other. She would not have known now Had it been Left to me. Marriage Laws don't make men.

As soon as I got my Gun, I made Good use of it. In two years I shot 300 hares Besides what I assisted in Killing with others in nets. To show you how I Troubled the Game-preserving Class, I was Fined £8 for Killing Hares. So I Flew away and the Debt still stands. I was fined £3 for Killing Hares another time, 5 pounds for killing without a Licence. This was a Revinue Prosecution and When I appealed to Sir George Gray nearly fifty years ago, he sent a reply: 'I see no Grounds to interfere with the Due Course of the Law.'

So much for the Sacred Game. There is no Man in England who Run more Risks, Been in more Dangerous Scrapes than me. Yet the only time I have Been in Prison was Not for Poaching but for getting a Poor Old widow woman a Bundle of Sticks as she had no coal. A Man who still Lives told the Keepers I had a Gun. It was a Long Piece of Ash, and they knew this Oadby man had told a Lie. But they sent me to Leicester Gaol for seven Days. They just thought it was time I was there. Ever Since then I have Poached with more Bitterness against the Class. If I am able, I Will Poach Till I Die.

III
POLITICS AND BICYCLING

There is no small difference between the Farmer of toDay and the farmer half a century ago. A man who Still Lives—he is in his 88th year—came to me once to say he Had a House full of Kids and no money. 'Jim', he said, 'If I don't get something towards the rent for old Bowlings, I shall Have the sack. He told me last week, though, that if I Had only five shillings, I could satisfy Him'.

'I ain't got a rap', I said, 'but I'll go and find a Hare. That'll make four shillings. Then I might be able to put a bob on to that an' there you are.'

I told him to stay at home while I went out shooting. He did so. But first he went out and Came Back with the news that Old Farryan—that's the farmer—was at work Raking Stubble in the field where the Hares were. 'Dare you go?' he asked.

'Yes,' I replied. I went out into the Field, took the Gun from my Pocket and Killed a Hare. Then I walked up to Farryan and told him how this man was situated. I found a soft Place in his Heart. He said, 'Get away. Don't let my Son know or it won't matter what I says.'

Poor old soul! If there's a Heaven I hope he's there. This was the pleasantest half hour I Spent in My Life. If you can't enjoy yourself by Doing good, Don't try by Doing Harm.

Mr. Bunny the Farmer was no worse. I shot a Hare on his land as He came through a Gate Close to me. I had the Hare in my Hand. 'I ain't fair got you this time,' he said. 'Now I shall Have you Down Leicester Gaol way.' He spit and Hit his stick on the Ground. He was Red Hot. But I laughed at Him and that made Him worse. But Hasty short-tempered men are always the Best to Deal with. 'You shocking scoundrel,' he shouted. 'This is a nice thing to laugh about.' But I knew that if I Could only get him to Stay a few minutes I would humour him. You can win more by kindness than by Abuse.

'Now, Mr. Bunny,' I said. 'I know you want to Do

Me. Why? I've never known you Do anyone Before, not even a Boy. If you Do me now, everybody will Hate You. You've a Good Name in the place. Don't lose it for a Petty Hare.'

He walked about, Struck his stick on the ground, spit a time or two and then said, 'Well, Darn you. Be off.' 'Never let me see you here again,' he shouted as I made off. How many of such men are left today? None.

Soon afterwards I made for Northampton rather than pay a Fine of £8 which I owed. When I reached King's Thorpe Hollow on the outside of the Town, I saw a Notorious Poacher Speaking from a Bedroom window. He was not a Poacher of game but a Poacher on the Privileges of the rich Class. His name was Charles Bradlaugh.

He was the Greatest, most fearless of Democrats that I ever knew. I never left that man—Politicaly —till Death parted us. I was in all his Struggles. When they kicked him out of Parliament I helped to put him Back. I will not trouble you with the details. I could fill this Book with tales of him.

When I left Northampton in 1880 and Returned to Leicester Mr. Grimson, a Great Radical, Came to my House. 'Mr. Hawker,' he said, 'you are still on the Register. Can you go and Vote for Bradlaugh? I have Bought 4/- to pay your Fare.'

'I don't want Paying,' I said. 'If I Couldn't get there any other way I would walk. But I have a Horse in the Front Room. It's called a Bicycle.'

The old Gentleman smiled. He left the next morning. By then my wife had made me a Rosette as Large as a Plate with Charley's Colours. By ten o'clock my vote was Recorded, for the last time. Bradlaugh was a Man without an Equal.

I strolled one Sunday evening into a Pub called the Admiral Nelson, on the Green, kept by George Craddock, and I found there what I did not like. There were Hard working men Spending their hard earned money in Exsesive Drinking. Good Fathers, Good Husbands, they were, but for this Failing, and all for the want of some greater attraction.

I am not going to Condem drink. I might as well Condem My Gun Because some men Blow out their Brains. I admire a man or Woman who advocates Temperance but I don't always approve of the manner in which they do it.

You cannot make a man Sober by force. Don't try. A man has as much Right to Drink as we have to abstain. This is a free country. We should allow everyone the same Liberty that we enjoy ourselves.

Let me Show you my mode of Business. These men would Fill with their wives and Little Children a large Clubroom. Men who with their wives' assistance could earn 14 Shillings per Day at finishing Boots were there. Most of them was like me. They went Field Rambles and did much Fishing. I soon became acquainted with some of them. But Beer Pals, Drink Birds of a Feather, all Flock together. I was always Ready to join any Party who stole a march on the rich Class by Poaching or Fishing. But not Drinking. As long as we do that we are strengthening the Hands of our Enemy and weakening our own.

At eight o'clock on Sundays, a Glass mug was Filled with whiskey and Handed round the Room. Anyone could drink but if you Did you would be Expected to Fill it first. Many a man drank not because he wanted to but because he did not want Others to Consider him Green. They never drew me into this Trap. And at turning out time, I have seen these poor men and their wifes past the Bounds of Man and Womanliness.

At that time Bicycling was all the Rage. I asked these men if they would assist me in Starting a Cycle Club so that we could Roam instead of sitting Here drinking. Without demanding any more Details, it was Done. We paid half a crown each, per week. When £8 was put together a Draw took Place and the Owner who picked the Right Number had the First Machine. The Manufacturer, Mr. Godley of Northampton, provided machines for men to Learn on. That so Delighted them that in a few weeks many had purchased their own. In twelve months we Paid to the Waterloo House 105 pounds for uniforms. That club grew to 185 members. When I left Northampton in 1880 I was made Captain against my will. For that Robbed me of a few hours Poaching. But I accepted that Proud Position and when I left I was Presented with a Beautiful Time-Piece which reminds me of the Pleasant Days during five years of the Rovers Bicycle Club. The men's wives sent my wife a Beautiful Tea Pot. If in our old age we may have to take a Cup of Tea from it without any Sugar, it will Taste Sweet.

You would have been surprised to see the Change in these men. They gained a Greater Respect for themselves, their Wives and their familys. Nothing on earth can do so much as Kind Words. You can often Lead a man when you Can't Drive him. Force is no Remedy. Since I left they sent me word they had Dined in the Spa Gardens at Leamington with the Speaker of the House of Commons, (Peel).

I returned to Leicester in 1880 and left Poaching for a while. Again my attention was Drawn to Cycling. Riding at this Period was all the go. At Aylestone Ground and at Belgrave, the People of

Leicester nearly went mad with Excitement. We had in Leicester two Champions of the world on the Tall Machine. They were Fred Wood and Dick Howell and for some time Leicester was Kept alive by the performances of these Cracks. They Defeated all comers. My eldest son joined these men and became a very fast rider, travelling all over England and Scotland with them. They went to Great Events at Wolverhampton, Molineaux Ground, the Greatest Centre for Sport and most attractive. They gained the Greatest Prizes.

Three important events took place here every year at Easter, Whitsuntide and at Bank Holiday. Lasting Monday, Tuesday and Wednesday, There was a mile championship, a mile Handicap, a four miles Consolation Race and others. My reason for perusing this matter is to Show a Little of the Vilany Behind the Screen called Sport.

I never was a Gambler because the Game was against me. If you Doubt this, read about the Turf Scandal which cost £60,000. I have been behind the Curtain, for i Trained and I Had Chances very few other men Had of being in the know. The great Champion of the World, Fred Wood, who Has Travelled and Rode in almost every Clime, would often Let me know what others would Like to know, but he could not entice me to gamble. What I might win today, I might Loose tomorrow, Let it alone. When I have told you what i intend to tell you, Phraphs you will see the Reason in my attitude.

When Living in Northampton, Fred Wood was a Pal to my Son. He was Living with his Mother, and Drawing a very small wage. He was a Bore Maker, and the Lad Done his Best for his Mother to keep a home above their Heads. When I formed the Rovers Club my Son joined them. Then he Lost him Has a Pal. For the Poor Lad Wood was not able to get a machine to join him for some time though I Done what I could to help him. When he got a second Hand bike for £4-10, he Looked Like a Tall man on a Small Donkey. We called him King Dick. He had very Large Limbs and he was always Racing men on the Roads. I made the Remark once that 'He'll be a Hot one some Day.' My words Proved True. He came to Leicester and Lodged with my Son soon after becoming Champion. He is now in or near newcastle but he always inquires about me.

I Have se Bare Faced villany in this sport. I know a young man in Northampton who was Favourite for Wolverhampton Handicap at Easter. The prize was £35. A Bookmaker gave him £40 not to try. He kept this man for his Book and when he was Becoming very Hot Favourite and most of the other Bookmakers Closed there Books against him, this man kept his open and took all he could in the three Days. That man would win nearly 100 pounds.

They Don't Stand to lay shillings Here but quids. i never se so much money Change Hands. I Have se nearly 20,000 people in the Ground. Once when I was in the Dressing Room, four men was going to Run in one Heat. One stood eight to one, another four to one and the other even money. They sent out of the Dressing Room four Half Quids to Back the man at eight to one and Let him win. You may say that the Book-maker would suspect there was something Crooked, but all villany suits these men in the end. For there is always so many Backing the Favourite.

IV

SOME NARROW SHAVES

As I was so busily Engaged in politics, there have been times in my life when I almost Forgot about Poaching. But I had many Narrow Shaves that I must State Here.

In 1871 I was living by the side of a Family where the Father was out of work and the Mother Heart broken. They had no Hope and not much Food. The husband was a Good Man but a fool. When he Drew his wages in times when work was plentiful, he would spent the surplus—after paying his wife—in Drink. The Poor Children could not Help and thousands

of men do the same. One Friday after everything in the house had been Pledged and there was
not a hope of a Dinner for Sunday, I said 'Can't you
Poach?'

'I would if I could,' he said, 'but I've nothing to
poach with.'

'Come with me tomorrow,' I said, 'and i will take
you to Kettering Shoot. We'll kill six Hares and you
can sell three for twelve shillings. I will find you
some food for a day or two.'

His wife was afraid. The Poor creature had no
Heart. She was Beat. But I promised her he would
Run no Risk. 'I'll do that.'

She consented and we went, I taking with me a
very Small Rifle that made but little noise. When
we got to Kettering, we made for a village called
geddington. I took him into a pub for he Had no
money, and we had half a pint each.

Now to work. I shot Number one Hare. Then
Number Two. A keeper saw all this. Then he came
out of Hiding.

My pal saw him, took the two hares and made for
home. The keeper came after me. But the further
he run the more Room there was between us. I run
towards the village and stole into an Empty Pig Sty.
I hid my Rifle and thought myself quite safe. But an
old woman saw me and told the Keeper. I am not
the first man who has been betrayed by a woman.

He and others seized me and took me to the Head
Keeper's House in the Park close by. Father and
two sons were washing their Guns. After reporting
his case, the Keeper said: 'His gun must have been
thrown away. We'll go and search for it.' He added:
'If I Had not seen him poaching, he'd have killed
all we've got.'

A young woman was getting tea and I asked her
for a Drink. She curtly replied: 'You'll have plenty
of water when you get to Kettering Lock-up. And
maybe there'll be some bread with it.'

But I thought to myself 'I'm not there yet.'

A policeman was sent for and he put handcuffs on
both my wrists. The Father told his youngest son
to go with the Bobby. When I heard this I looked
around at him. He was wearing a heavy suit of
Clothes, heavy boots, and as I intended to Have a
Dash for Liberty on my way to Kettering, I thought
my Chance was not a Bad one.

When we reached a Lane to the left by Earl
Barton (or Barton Teagrave, I'm not sure) now for
it. It was a Beautiful course ahead. I could see for
400 yards. No one was about. 'Policeman,' I said.
'Will you Loose one of my Handcuffs. I can't go
any further, or I shan't be very Pleasant Company.'

He looked at the Keeper for his assent. He gave
him a Nod as much as to say 'I can catch him if he
Runs away.' But I knew better.

My Left Hand was liberated and the handcuffs
left on my right hand. Then down the lane I ran at
a Rate I could have kept up any Length of time. I
just put on a spurt to get clear, then I slackened to
a nice steady pace. After running 200 yards I had
a peep at them. The Bobby was a long way behind.
He was pulling his coat off. In fact he had shot his
bolt.

The Keeper was about 30 yards behind. He was
Running above Upright, not a good sign for an
Athlete. He was Bringing his great Boots down to
make a great noise. It wasn't the pace that killed,
it was the weight he was carrying.

Then I saw danger ahead. Two men were leading
a cart with soil. Keeper shouted 'Stop him.' But the
men did not hear.

When I got near, one asked in an undertone,
'What 'ave yer done, mate?'

'Killed two Hares to feed Hungry Kids,' I said.

'Go on, lad,' he replied. 'You've got 'em beat.'

Now something happened I shall never Forget.
There was a Snowstorm. When I Bolted the Sun
was Shining Lovely. Then in a moment there was
Lumps of Snow as big as Hen's Eggs.

I turned to look back but could see no one. At
this point I found myself by a brook and a Bridge
crossed the road. I put my hand on the Fog-stone
and over I went in a moment and along the Side of

the Brook. Then I thought they would trace me in the Snow. After running 300 yards I came to a Large Spinney. In I went and at that moment the Sun Came out. In a few minutes Snow, Keeper and Bobby had all disappeared.

I sat down for I had made up my mind to go Back and Fetch my Rifle later on. I sat looking at the Hand Cuffs and wondering how I could get them off my other hand. To my Joy and Delight I discovered He had left the key in. I soon threw them off then.

When it was dark I went Back to Geddington in search of the Pig-sty. I found it and entered in search of my Rifle. As I got inside Two Men Nailed me. They had found my weapon and thinking I might Come Back to Fetch it, had contrived to wait for me. I was marched to Kettering Police Station by three men. They thought me unsafe with the two who had captured me. They told the Inspector not to Let me out but to keep me as a Dangerous Character.

But even in the Inspector I found a friend. Whatever you do in Life—even if it appears rough—let your motive be good and you will Find many Difficulties will be overcome. The Hedgehog is Rough and Full of prickles on the surface but take off his jacket and he is tender underneath. We must not judge by outward appearances.

The Inspector Came into my Cell. 'Young man,' he said. 'I will give you a chance. Tell me your address and I will wire at my own Expense. If it be found correct I will let you out.'

'Will you let me stay till morning?' I asked.

'Well,' said the Inspector, 'You're the First Man that asked me that question. They always like to get away.'

In the morning he gave me a Good Breakfast. It was the same sort he had himself. Then I thanked him and we parted for ever.

I had one or two more narrow escapes before I left Northampton. I was coming through Far Cotton, a little hamlet, when I saw Sergeant Gibbings coming towards me. I had a Hare and a Gun in my pocket. I opened a Front Door and walked into a man's house. They was having their Dinner. I told them how I stood and the man allowed me to Sit Down till the Bobby had gone away.

He knew I had game, but under the Poaching Prevention Acts, they have no Power to arrest only on the Highway. When I went into that House it might Have Proved a Trap. It is Better to be Born Lucky than Rich. I gave the man one shilling who Sheltered me. A man may poach a considerable time if he is not known by the Police. But when they know you, they are always on to you.

While living at New Duston three miles from Northampton, I could stand making Boots and see Pheasants walking about And sometimes Hanging in the Same Room I was in! I was living on the borders of Earl Spencer's estate. A man of the name of John Miller would sometimes Come into my Shop. He kept a Gun Hanging up in his House but I never seed him use it. One day he said, 'I should like to go with you some morning and kill a Hare. I have a Gun.'

'You can go next Sunday morning,' I said, 'but you'll have to be up before it's light. When I go out for a morning shoot, I don't go to Bed but sit in some snug place till nearly peep of day. Then I go and secrete myself and wait for prey. There is more Hares killed by Poachers at the Peep of Day than at anytime. But you want to know their Habits first. I have stood at one Spot and killed five Hares in twenty minutes almost before it was Light.

On Saturday night this man prepared for going out with me by getting nearly Drunk. This was to give him Courage for we was going where it was Rather Warm. But if you don't go in such places you don't find much to fetch. I planted him where I knew Hares would pass him. Then I went and sat 100 yards away. As soon as it was Light four Hares passed him into Haseleston Heath, a large wood. Yet not a shot was fired. I went up to him and found him fast asleep. Drink had Robbed him of four Hares. Had I been there, I should have had the lot.

Once instead of going to Leicester Station for Fear the Police might be waiting for me, I walked to Glen Station, took my ticket for Northampton and then found the Oadby Bobby Rushing at me. I was a bit too nimble. He run me up the Line and I knew all the time he would be second in the race. Soon I was walking to Northampton with the Ticket in my Pocket.

While living in Leicester, two of my pals went out Early for a morning Shot, but failed to get a thing. Coming home by the Abbey Park, Sergeant Ormiston stopped them and took their small Rifles. He snatched them out of their pockets by Force. Playing on the weakness and ignorance of these two men, he took their Rifles to the Police station. They came to ask me what Course to Pursue. 'Have him up Before the magistrates,' I said. 'Put in for Time wasted and Loss caused by being Deprived of your Rifles.' They sued him for fourteen shillings. Rather than face the music, he Paid it. If you had Been Bred in the country and you was Fond of a Gun, you would know a Little more than you Do about the County Police. My Greatest Surprise is that more are not shot.

On a Piece of Waste Land belonging to the Corporation of Leicester near Man's Farm,—where there was old brickyards—I have fired Thousands of Shots at Target Practise. No, My leisure time was not spent in pubs.

One afternoon after I had been Firing some time, two Police Officers appeared on the Scene. Fortunately, I saw them before they noticed me. I was standing on a Sloping Bank. So I placed my Little Rifle—20 inches Long—behind me and laid down on it.

When the Police came to me they just stood and looked.

'Have you seen anyone shooting about Here?' they asked.

'I've just been watching a young Man shooting,' I said, 'but he's gone. I Fancy he must be in the garden on the Other side of that Hedge.'

Away they went and I Did Not Stop Them. Nor did I stay on the Bit of Waste Land.

One of the Finest Shots I Have ever made in my Life was out of a 21 inch Martini Henry Barrell. These Barrells you could purchase from Birmingham for five shillings Each and cutting the Heavy End to two Feet, make a useful Bit of Kit for a Poacher.

I have one today—rather than the Long Barrell the Army uses. We use a small one at 50 to the

Pound. One ounce of Powder makes a Hundred Charges and that will send a Bullet through a Hare 100 yards away. But the Bullett must Fit in the Breech and the Breech be air-tight and large enough to let the bullett cut its way out. We saw the Barrell off, put the Powder in, Breach Ball on the Top, give it a tap and then it is ready for use.

One calm day with not a breath of wind, I put a four inch target on a clear clay bank 100 yards away. Then I lay down on my Belly and had one shot. I loaded again and took exactly the same aim. Then I went to look at the Result.

I could only find one hole. It was two inches below the target. I Dug the Bullett out and found the two welded together. I will give any man a shilling if he can seperate them with his hands.

It was The finest weapon the army ever had for accuracy but perhaps the Lee Milford travels Farther.

I was walking one morning round Evington, close to Mr. Cooper's house. Not twenty yards from his parlour sat a Hare grazing. I thought I should like a Pop at it. As far as I could see it was only 200 yards away.

So having no higher sight than 100, I took it Rather Full. That is, I se a little more of the Fore Right of the animal.

It was a wet morning—just what the poacher

likes when there's not many people about. I lay the
rifle on a Stump in the Hedge and got nice and
steady. I knew the Rifle would play its part if only
I played mine. How grand it is when you can put
your Trust in anything.

I steadily pressed the Trigger and I see the bullett
spin the wet up, a few yards beyond the Hare. She
dropped for a second. Then before I had loaded
again, she was feeding. I knew I could settle her now.
I took sight again and after pressing the Trigger, I
saw the Hare turning somersaults. Over and over she
went. Surely some one will see her, I thought, for
the House was so near. How I wished I had killed
her Dead. What am I to do, I wondered, if she goes
on turning over and over?

Then Mr. Cooper came out of the house with his
coachman. They walked down the coach drive on to
the lane where I stood smoking my pipe. They had
not seen the hare.

When they got to me, I said: 'Mr. Cooper, if you'd
been here a few minutes ago you'd 'ave seen a man
by your hedge firing a Rifle.'

He turned to his man, saying 'That's just what
we heard.' 'Which way has he gone?'

'Towards Evington,' I told them.

'Come on, this way,' he shouted as they both ran
after him.

It was not long before I Done the same. But I

went to the hare first, which was still turning over; I pushed her in my pocket alive and when I got clear, had a look at her. The bullett had gone through her neck, but a little too high to kill. She would soon have died from loss of blood. But I killed her to prevent that.

V

ANOTHER NEAR THING

Some ten years ago I went with a young man to a watermill and we found a large number of waterhens there. He said 'It's quite safe here.'

But after a few shots, I found that it would have been safer to stay at Home. 'The miller's coming,' cried my pal.

He was. He was a tall young man, with Legs Like Line Props. We got a very good start or we might have fared worse. After running nearly half a mile, my Pal said: 'Jimmy, I'm about done.'

The pace was not very Fast, but just fast enough to keep on even terms with the miller.

'Keep straight on', I told him, 'and I'll turn off to the right. I'll make 'im believe I'm licked.'

I knew that as I had the rifle in my hand, the miller was sure to follow me.

My plan worked. When I inclined to the right, the miller crossed towards me, saving quite a lot of ground at the corner. I had a good hundred yards in Hand, but that's not much if you have a man after you and he is 150 yards Better. I kept straight on and found He Had Had enough. I soon proved this. For I Dropped to a walk. So did he. Maybe he was thinking 'I shall be with you by and by.' He little thought what I had up my sleeve.

First I had a Peep towards my Pal. He was out of all Danger. After walking about twenty yards with my Eyes on him, the miller, I noticed, broke into another 'jig-jog.' I walked till he got within thirty yards of me. Then I showed him what Deception there is in life. I was then close upon 60 years of age, but I could run!

If you would like to be able to do what I done, you must have plenty of fresh air. The more you get of that the Longer you will live. And try to do with little drink if you possibly can. I have never in the whole of my life been the worse for Drink.

VP-E

I have said Before that no man has been in more Danger and Suffered less than I have done. I have lost but one Long Net and one Rifle, that splendid little weapon that once belonged to an Oadby man, Richard Newby who has Long gone to his Last Home.

One night me, Jack Wright and Walter Greenfield, Brother of the noted Alf Greenfield, the Birmingham Boxer, went to a wood six miles from Northampton, called Nobottle. It is on Earl Spencer's estate. We had always agreed that if any one come out at us, we would make for the Centre of the Netting.

I put my Net Down First, Greenfield did his next and Jack last of all. So you see we were nicely seperated when out Burst the Keepers.

As soon as I heard them Shout, me and Jack met in the centre but Walter instead of standing there or coming towards us Bolted into the Middle of the Field and the Keepers Got him. Seeing how things stood Jack run up to his net in the hopes of getting it up. Then we noticed they had Disabled Walter with a cut Down the front of the Head.

I Dropped quietly into the Dyke to watch Further Events. It was a very Dark night. In a few minutes three keepers came along pulling up the nets. If they had had a dog it would have been all over with me. He would have smelt me.

I sat half an hour till everything was quiet. Then

I went to where we began to net. I had hid nine Rabbetts and a Hare what we had caught at Harpole Hills. My pals did not know I had had the presence of mind to hide them, but I thought 'you never know what is going to Happen!'

I seed no more of Jack but Expected Walter was safely captured. So I made my way to New Duston. I had a Sister living there and on my way home I saw a light so I went up the Back Way and when I got in there sat Jack. But he had no net.

After a little time someone approached the door. It was Walter, covered with Blood. His Forehead had been split open. After they Had knocked him Silly they left one Keeper with him while the other three went to Look for the Netting.

After he came round Walter Jumped to his feet and kicked the Keeper in his Private part and for weeks this man's life was in danger. Then he escaped. Had he stood his ground it would have been a mery time for a few minutes for he was a very Powerful man. He could have done in two men himself. Keepers are Tinkers if you stand your ground. I have proved that above once. If you can get away without loss, do, but Stand if you Can't.

I knew what would happen. So I was fully prepared next day when there came a tap at the door. When nearly captured a few hours before, I had a little hair on my Face and especially on my Top Lip. Now I had made sure it had disappeared. Then I put on my white apron and started work in my little Ill-furnished front room, driving Brass Rivetts into Boots I was making for French and German soldiers marching to Slaughter.

My wife answered the knock at the door. It was the Bobby I had got away from at Northampton. I went on hammering away at my work and left the wife to do the Talking. They are better at that than men. Every minute I expected to Hear him say, 'That's him.'

But he didn't. Either he did not know me or he would not. At last the Sergeant asked, 'Have you any lodgers?'

'We had one for a few weeks,' I answered. 'It was my brother. But my wife grew Tired of his ways. He wouldn't work. He was always in the fields Poaching or anything. He's been taken for me many times. But he wears a Little Hair on the Face. If he gets into trouble, you won't catch him, cos' he can run like a Hare. At last my wife could stand him no more and she told him to go. He reckoned to go off to Kettering. I expect he's there now.'

The police looked at one another. Then they muttered a few Words and Bid us Good Day. I never heard no more.

VI

IN THE SEASON OF THE YEAR

On the First of September, one Sunday morn,
I shot a hen pheasant in standing corn
Without a licence. Contrive who can
Such a cluster of crimes against God and man.
                              RICHARD MONCKTON,
                              1st Lord Houghton.

During my twenty years in Northampton I Done a
Deal of Long Netting. This is the most deadly net
used for the destruction of Game. I will describe it.

Not that it is always safe to believe all you Read.
But I will Defy any man to Prove this untruthful. I
once saw in the 'Illustrated Sporting Dramatic' an
article called 'The Life of a Poacher.' The writer

described the Pleasure it gave him to watch by the Light of the Moon his Dog bringing rabbits into a Long Net.

It made me Laugh. I don't say all this was not true, but the man was not a Poacher. If he was, then I've never met one. Like him I've been in at the Death of Thousands of Hares in these last forty years. Yet never in my life have I seen one Rabbit Drove into a net whether by man or dog. For a man who knows his trade will select the Darkest night possible for his work. I have known men leave off when the stars appeared, for Rabbits are best killed by Feeling. A Dark Night, and a Dry wind that is not too strong, that is the night for killing Rabbits. I have helped to net every wood worth going to within ten miles of Northampton. Several times I have been to woods twelve miles from the town. Around Daventry I knew every inch of ground from my boyhood days. Many times four of us would take train for Weedon and then walk to Badly Wood three miles away, sell our stuff in Daventry before daylight and no one would be any the wiser, only the man who Bought from us.

When we have sat down and had a rest after Killing as many hares as we could carry, I have thought of the man who owned that wood. He was a Red Hot Tory who travelled 68 miles to the House of Commons—to trespass on my liberty.

So this was Tit for Tat. I was getting a bit of my own back on Sir Charles Knightly Bart., who sat in the House for 30 years and never opened his Kisser. He was a Magistrate on the Daventry Bench and I have held his horse and led it out for four hours and he has given me twopence.

Fifty years ago Mr. Thomas Glover, a Farmer of Oadby, came to my Wife's Father and said 'Jim, if you Chaps don't come and kill the Hares on the Evington Foot Road, they'll eat all my Barley.'

Four men went and in three nights they killed nearly 30 Hares. If they had had the long net they would have done the lot in one night. But the nets they used were Pieces made to cover a Gate four yards wide and to cover a Gap and open space, and small Purse Nets to cover a Run. If a Hare gets in one of these nets, most that comes out from the same hole gets away.

Not so with the Long Net. Nothing escapes from it. I have caught Deer, Fox, Badger, Cat, Hare, Rabetts, Hedgehogs and once I caught a Policeman. We was sitting across a footroad and Bobby walked straight into our net near Hardingstone. But he was soon out of it and off. I was very glad. We didn't want to capture him. He was a Police Sergeant. Had he stayed I don't know what might have Happened. There was six of us and I think he knew it.

[49]

Long nets are of different lengths. If you are going to work with a Party, a net 75 yards long may be enough. If you have one a 100 yards long, you would have to do more work During the night and only take your share of the spoil. But if you Lived and Worked a good deal by yourself has I have, the Longer your net the Better.

When six men are going out with a net 75 yards long, number one poacher peggs his net Down at the Start with a Short iron peg. Then away you all go in Front of the wood or spinney. When number one has run his net out 75 yards, Pull it rather Tight and Stick another iron peg in the ground to keep it so. There the net Lays Ready for Pegging up with Eight Long Pegs you have in a Long Coat Pocket.

Now you begin to peg it up. As you do this the other five men go and Do the same. The net when set would be forty inches high or more, according to a man's taste. There would be 75 yards of line top and bottom and if a good net, 120 yards of netting— if the net was tight and lacking what we call Bagging or Loose netting. If it was not Baggy, the net would not kill. Prey would hit against it and Bounce Back, but when they strike the loose net, the Bagging covers them and the more they struggle the worse for them. They are killed by Feeling, as I have said before.

By keeping your hand on the Top Line of the Net

you know when they strike the net. Then when you go to where he is in, you find that the weight of his body has pulled the Top Line down. Stoop down and you will see him.

When every net is set, Number six signals to number five who tells four who signals to number three and so on. Number one Lets the Dog go then and the sport Commences. The most I have ever been at the Death of was 188 Rabbets and 3 Hares, at a place called Salcey Forrest, crown lands seven miles from Northampton on the Olney Road. It always seemed strange to me that if you see 100 Hares come out of a wood, it don't matter where, we never get them in. They won't stop to Feed among Rabbetts but go Further afield because of the Smell. Nothing smells worse than Rabbetts.

I walked one afternoon near Northampton along an old green lane called Danes Camp. On one Side there is a Large Spinney, at the bottom a Beautiful Spring always Running. After having a Drink and a smoke, I thought 'What a Lovely Place for a Pheasant.'

I had never seen one there. But I took from the Bank a Little Soil, added some water and made what the kids call Pudding. I knew if a Pheasant was in that Spinney he would come there to Drink before he went to Roost.

[51]

When i Came Back i Could trace his Little Footprints in the mud. So next morning I was up at 1.30 a.m., before it was Light soon after 2.30.

Gipsy vans was usually found in this Lane. I had to pass them. However, I crept by as quiet as I Could. I could hear men, women and Children Snoring under the vans and surrounded by Canvas. When I got to the last van I heard the Growl of a very Large Dog Letting me know that he was not asleep. But he made no great noise. Gipsies don't often have Noisy Dogs. Still waters run Deep.

When i Reached the Spring I Dropped into a Deep Dyke, Laid my gun on the Bank and waited for Daylight. A Pheasant, like Many Men, is very fond of Drink, but it must be Clean or He will not have it. What a Beautiful Example the Pheasant sets, for many Men will Drink any Filth if it only bears a certain Name. But if there is no Clean Water you won't find Pheasants. They will Roam till they find it.

At Peep of Day I saw the figure of a man crossing the water where I had come. He stopped within twenty yards of me and took from under his coat a small bantam cock. He set it on the ground Pegged to a Line, gave it a little Corn and then Dropped in the Same Dyke I was in. I could not understand this.

After eating a little corn the cock began to crow.

Instantly a pheasant answered from a long way off.
'Now I know your little game,' I told myself. 'You're
going to entice the pheasant near and then shoot it.'

But I was wrong. Meantime I put my Gun to the
shoulder and waited as the bantam crowed again
and a pheasant answered from a few yards away.
Then the Proud Bird stepped forward into the Lane,
I pressed the trigger and he fell Dead.

The man sat still not knowing who I was. I went
out and picked up the pheasant. Then I looked at
the Bantam. He was wearing a four-inch steel spur
on each foot. When the bird met a pheasant in com-
bat, he would soon have pierced his opponent. Then
the man would come out and pick up the pheasant.
Now I knew his secret.

I Dropped my Bird on the ground, took my Gun
apart and put it into my Pocket. When he saw me
do that the man came out for he knew I was a
Poacher. Keepers never do that. But he came forward very Reluctantly, a little old Black-eyed man,
nearly eighty years of age, I should say, to judge
from his looks. I says to him: 'Dad, this is Dog rob
Dog. Give me a shilling and take the Bird. Or I'll
give you a bob and keep it.'

Then he sulkily spoke. 'Give me the shilling. I can
have a pheasant any time.'

I walked back with him to his caravan. When we
parted I wished I was a Gipsy.

VII
ENCOUNTERS WITH ANIMALS

How Grand is The Life of a Poacher. Yet it is more Grand to Learn the Habbits of Game. you Learn something more of the works of our Creator, for we find examples set it would be well if many of us would try to imitate. If you went for a walk and Se a Hare Travel a Certain Road, he will Travel the same way the next evening if He Had Not been Disturbed, and Come Back the same way in the morning. In the winter they travel a Long way in Search of Food. If you was to Stand has i Have Done Hundreds of times before it is Light, the

First Sound you would Hear Before Daylight would be the Lark. About a quarter of an Hour before Daylight you will Hear the Sound High up in the air. As a Poacher, Look up—a Hare will be on you almost Before you can se it. If you are Standing where he Has to Travel you must Learn this. What Has told the Hare it is time he was away? The Lark.

i once went to a Gate that Led on to a Clover Field near Northampton where it was to Hot to use a Gun. I Stood quietly at the Side of a Tree and when i Heard the Lark before it was Light, sixteen Hares Passed me. If the Road Had not been white with Dust I should have been unable to se them. All these Passed me in twelve minutes. I Stood for Half an Hour but no more. This is a Proof that they Listen for the Lark.

A Hare is very Sensitive to Smell or Sound. It don't Depend on sight so much. If you can see one coming straight towards you and you stood still, she would go straight by you, but if you only moved or drew your Breath Heavily, she would hear you in an instant. They can smell very quick. I was standing one morning when one came towards the Turnpike. I was smoking and I knew she hadn't se me. But the wind was blowing from me to her and when she got 60 yards away, she stopped, stood up on her hind legs for a second and then went through the hedge and came out on the road about the same Distance behind me. I never used any more Tobacco till I had done my work.

What proved more interesting to me was tracing the Little Footprints in the Snow. Before a Hare creeps in to a Resting Place for the Day, it tries to deceive man. If you Trace a hare and reach the place where it is lying, you suddenly lose the track. Then stand and get your gun ready. She is bound to be within Gun Shot but she may be behind you. They jump up to ten yards twice or three times. Who has learnt them to do this? If She gets up and you don't kill her, let your pal follow her. She will take you miles, then come back to where you put her up. This is her house. Stand there as I have done and you will kill Her. I Traced one into a garden and to get out or face me, the animal would have had to cross a Brook six yards wide. At the bottom end the Brook was frozen over with thin ice and covered with Snow. But she knew the Brook was there. When I got in the Garden away she went over the Brook. We measured her jump. It was twenty-five feet. As soon as she landed on the other side I tipped her over. She had been there before.

The fox and stoat are curious Little Chaps. One eats a lot he Don't kill, the other kills a Lot he Don't eat. Many people think the Fox kills a large quantity of Game. He don't. He is too lazy. I never knew many men do much Hard work if they were a bit foxey. But a fox will Devour the Best Food if he happens to find it, perhaps in a snare or net, or perhaps wounded or sickly. They prowl about on the look-out for anything. But they kill a large quantity of fowls and ducks, not because they are better to eat but because they are easier to kill. They kill more by day than night and many times they Hide [nearby in the day?].

I was in the fields once not far from a Farmhouse. I se the end of a Fowl's wing poking through the Ground. I pulled it out and found it was still warm. I took it home and my wife Put him in the oven without a word of complaint.

Once I was waiting for a Rabbit to come on land where I had permission to shoot—from the Rev. Mr. Baines. I shot a rabbit but did not kill it. However, I knew it could not get away so when it crept into the Dyke I continued to stand until another came near and this I killed Dead. It was then getting dark. I went to pick up number two and then went to look for number one. A fox sat eating it, as Contented as could be. He Had Heard the first shot, and then came to try his Luck and found the injured rabbitt. He had eaten the Best Part of it. Then he merely crawled away, as much as to say 'I've had the Best part of it; you're welcome to the Rest.'

Had my gun been loaded he would not have had much to grin about.

Nothing on four legs kills as many head of game as the little Stoat. But he rarely eats what he kills. He plays the part of a Sanitry Officer. Where rabbets are too thick on the ground, they are like the Human Family and get Disease. This little chap keeps them down or Regulates them. How Beautiful are the works of nature.

Some years ago when the Rabbets was very Thick on Mr. Prentice's land I killed more diseased than Healthy animals. When you buy a rabbett, look at its Liver. If diseased, they have a mite-Tick all over; if Healthy they are clear. If you was to kill one today, you'd find them as clear as a bell, because they are not so thick. What a lesson for us all to learn.

When a stoat does eat a rabbet, it just eats the Brain. It does so when the weather is very Still, with not much wind. Now I'll tell you what I mean. The Stoat Feeds on Small Birds and when there is no wind they Roost High. On very Rough Nights they roost Down nearly on the ground. Then it is that the stoats' get their harvest. Many a time I have been Sitting when a stoat passed me with a bird Fluttering in its mouth.

In the Spring most pheasants leave the woods for

Breeding quarters. If you can find a small Plantation within two miles or more of any Preserve, it
don't matter if there is only half a dozen trees, so
long as there is water near, you will find a Brace or
a couple of Brace of Pheasants. But they don't breed
in this little Spinney. They prefer a Field or two
fields not far away, perhaps in the Corn or grass Or
in anything that will conceal them. When disturbed
whether by man or Dog, they Fly into the spinney
for refuge.

When the Hen has laid her eggs—from twelve to
twenty—she begins to Sit. The cock bird will visit
her many times during the day and keep all day
long talking to her. I could tell you to a few yards
where a hen was sitting. For when a cock is far from
her he speaks Louder. When He gets close to her
He speaks Low. I Heard one a few years ago speaking very Low and I went and looked in the hedge
bottom at the side of the Brook between the sewage
farm and the allotments. There I found the Hen on
sixteen eggs. When I disturbed her she made for
the Little Spinney on Wigston Lane against Wash
Brook. I broke one, but they had been sat on too
long or I would have made fourpence each. So I
covered up the eggs so that no one would Find them
and when hatched the hen took the young into the
Spinney.

When the Eggs are Hatched, they don't take the

young into the Woods Direct. They keep them out as Long as they possibly can do. I have known the keepers come out with Dogs and drive them back into the woods and many times they have Drove me at the same time. Why don't they send them back to the woods direct? The answer is that to enable the young to grow strong, they keep them in the Fields so that they are more able to Resist any Attack from their common enemy, which include the Fox, Badger, Polecat, House Cat, Stoat, Magpie, Hawk. All these are common enemies but the worst of the lot is the Domesticated Cat. She has such patience. A Cat will sit for hours and never move, but when it does it is not often that it makes a mistake. A magpie will attack the eyes of the young if they are taken back to the woods as soon as they are hatched. All would soon be anihillated. What a Beautiful example the Pheasant sets us. Do we look after the Little Ones till they are able to look after themselves? I wish we did.

If you was to go into some woods I have been in, you would not go many yards before finding a sitting pheasant. After you'd had a pop at him, the bird would go on sitting. Then you stumble on the truth. This is a Dummy. The pheasant is made of wood and no man in the night would ever distinguish it from a real one, unless he put his teeth into it. You may be inclined for another Shot. But the next one too, may be a dummy. So between Hope and Fear you come out and get away while you have the chance. The Keepers may have heard the shot. Some Keepers make a dummy with a loose neck which blows in the wind. That makes you feel sure the Dummy is real, but you have a Pop at him with the same result.

In old Dukes Wood which I have been in, you get about twenty yards and then find yourself caught in a Briar, you think. While looking around for a pheasant you give an extra pull to get clear and you Hear a very loud Report. It is an alarm Gun with one pound of powder. You may guess what the Report would be like. If the keepers lived four miles away they would hear it. A large piece of iron is driven into the Ground and a piece of iron the shape of a ring Runs Down this. It is pegged at the Top and this peg is connected with wires that cross every Riding and piece of open land in the wood. When you touch one it Lets Down the Ring into the Gun cap in a vessel with a Pound of Powder in, similar in shape to a coffe pot. This stands on the ground. The ring would be four pounds in weight. When the Keepers find that no one has been, they pick up the vessel containing the Powder and put it away till another time.

When keepers Breed pheasants under Fowls— as many do—all the eggs they find in the fields where they dont think it would be Safe to Leave them, they bring home. If you walk round Stoughton you will se Boxes with Fowls sitting on Pheasant eggs. When they are a certain age they take them up, and put them in Spinneys that are not very Large. When we get to know this, we go and clear them out. I Have Done a Lot of this in some Countys, but not in Leicestershire because i Have never se the Chance.

Now we will take a Spinney twenty yards wide and one hundred yards in length, get in the middle, take some fine wire and set every Hole across it. Don't miss one. It may take an Hour to do it. Well then come out, go to either end, and then walk Steadily Backwards and Forwards across it. If you go too fast they will take wing. When you get to the wires, kill and take the game out and Reset. Come away, Start at the other end, and you will Clear them all out.

You may say this is too Bad. Is it any worse than we have been served? We Had no voice in making the Game Laws. If we Had i would submit to the majority for I am a Constitutionalist. But I am not going to be a Serf. They not only Stole the land from the People but they Stocked it with Game for Sport, Employed Policemen to Look after it, neglected their Duty in Looking after Private Property, and Hundreds of Keepers got the Sack. And we the Toilers have to Pay the Piper.

Even the Farmer who Fed the Hare with his Produce was not allowed to kill a Hare till we got the Ground Game Act under a Liberal Government. You will remember how Mr. Thomas Glover came and told me when to kill his Hares, because he Dare not Do it himself. i Remember Powis Keck, Stoughton Hall, near Oadby, killing His Game. Then up Rose the Rents.

What do you think of the Poaching Prevention Act? If you was in Possession of a Rabbit on the Highway, it would not matter if you had found it there—a Policeman seeing it on you Has only to say 'I have Suspicions this man has been on Private land for this.' Then it's two months.

I have mentioned a Policeman who Lived in Oadby and who [had an adventure] with the Long Net. Once he went into Thomas Taylor's house in Oadby and Put Some Fowls' Feathers in his Pockit. Now Taylor, like me, was a Poacher and they was so embittered against him that this is how they served him. He had a Month in Leicester Gaol.

Yet his Mother stood in the House and se the Policeman do it. But they would sooner Believe the Police. Don't you think it is Enough to make men Rebel? If you knew what Some County Police are, you would say 'Yes'. Yet this man is now an Inspector. All my Life I Have Poached. If I am able, I will Poach till I Die.

VIII
CALLING THE HARE

Now I will come to the man who said 'Mr. Hawker, you are a very Honest Man'. I don't Remember being Called that before. When I Left Oadby the same as I Left my House—in a Hurry—i owed a small Debt of 12s -9d. After being away 30 years I went and Paid it to Mr. and Mrs. Sidars. Paying it was my greatest Pleasure; to some men it would have been the Greatest Punishment.

Now One word about calling the Hare. How many People Doubt this. I have convinced several by Proof. A Jack Hare can be called in March and April if the weather is suitable. A Doe Hare can be called at Harvest-time. When you Call a Hare in Spring, imitate the Doe. When calling at Harvest-time, imitate the young. A Jack Hare won't come at Harvest-time.

I was once in a smoke Room in Bridge Street, Northampton, where a young man was Listening to my claim. This man named Hall—he kept a Large Draper's shop—would not believe anything of the kind. He would lay any amount that I could not call up a Hare near enough to Shoot it. 'I never Gamble, but I'll tell you what we can do', I said. 'I will not only Call one up, but I will Shoot it with a Small Rifle'—which i was then Carrying in my Pockit—'if you will buy me a Pound of Gun Powder at three shillings. If I don't do it, I'll buy you a small Box of Cigars.'

We had to wait for a few weeks for it was then November. The time arrived and I took him to a farm with a Foot road leading through it. There were plenty of Hares there, but it was also a very warm place (Wooton, three miles from Northampton). We went at a time when the Keeper would be having his tea for in these matters, you must learn the Habbitts of men as well as Game. At about five o'clock, we walked to a Gate, Leading into a Wheat field. The wheat was hardly high enough to cover a Hare. I saw that a Hare lay about two hundred yards away.

Now I says, 'if you move, I won't pay.'

'I won't move,' says he.

Then I laid my Rifle on the Gate Post. He stood close behind me like a Soldier. I began to call. It was a Jack Hare and away he came. When he was within twenty-five yards, I stopped calling and the Hare stood up on his hind legs. I pressed the trigger and we could se the Bullett beat the soil up just round him. 'Jimmy,' says he, 'you've missed him.' Then the Hare ran about two yards and Dropped Dead. The bullett had gone strait through his Chest. I thought the young man would have went mad with Delight. 'You'll believe it now, won't you?' I says.

Once I was Calling while on Earl Spencer's estate. I had no Gun but was merely doing it to show a Friend of mine. I had three Hares and a Fox all around me. What did the Fox come for? He thought there was a Hare trapped in a wire. I was standing quietly calling one evening when a Keeper heard me. I saw him run all along one Hedge for he thought a Hare was in a snare.

Now for a Little Advice to the young poacher. On the boundaries of Game Preserves near to large towns, Keepers will get into a Spinney—particularly on Sundays—and watch for poachers. You don't think anyone is there. I have had many narrow escapes. If I think anyone is there, I hide myself, sit quietly and then they will come out to look for you. Never do anything at Random. I was once sitting watching for a Hare which I knew Travelled through this open Space. It was on Mr. Hodger's land. A Keeper saw me go and Plant myself. He tried to steal a march on me. Then I saw a white horse watching the Keeper. He must have been creeping towards me. As he moved, the horse did. I crept through the hedge and then saw old Sandy Hancock who still Lives within a hundred yards of me, exit.

There are many signs which have saved me in the past. If you want to go into a Spinney and you would like to be sure if any one is there, sit down, have a smoke and watch the crows. When they fly over you will soon know if anyone is in. Blackbirds too, tell you as quick as any bird. All these signs you must learn. If you want to escape Punishment, I shan't say, 'Don't poach', but do be careful.

IX
LOOKING BACK

When I came to live in dear old Oadby in 1890 I found many changes in the Place. I found in Wigston Lane a nice cemetery. And as I looked through it for names of men of usefulness who have left a Record, I found the names of men who had few opportunities but strong will-power and others who had ample opportunities and no will. We should not have known these men had ever lived if it had not been for the Stone which marks there Resting Place.

It was not Graves that brought me back to Oadby.

I came back to bring up to the Best of my ability two orphan children, one of them a cripple. Today these young women are able to Look after themselves.

At Different times the Guardians of the Poor would Pay me a visit in the interests of these Children. They was very pleased with what they saw. One of the Guardians, the Rev. J. Raine, saw my Gun Hanging up.

'Mr. Hawker, do you Shoot?' he asked.

'Yes, sir,' I replied.

'Then I give you Permission to go on my Land,' he said.

I Retained that Favour for Several years. Although me and this Gentleman was as far apart Politicaly has the Sun from the Moon, he never allowed that to Alter our Friendship. Very few men who are Extreme in their views Have a Kind word for a Minister of the Church of England. Even Logan, Labour M.P., was always making Bitter Attacks on these men. Yet there are some of the Best men in the Establishment and this man is one. For in Performing His Duty as a Guardian of the Poor, he follows the precepts of Christ. 'Feed my Lambs'.

There is so much attracting the attention of Different men today that I should like to Show you

Both Sides of Different Pictures Presented. i won't say that i am right; but if i am not i am willing to be Put Right. I am not going to Speak from what I Have Read or what I have been told, but from Personal Experience During 70 years.

A man we all know, a man i am not going to Speak Disrespectful of although we Differ—I refer to Joseph Chamberlain—thinks Tarriff Reform would Benefit us, especially the Farmer, by Putting a Tax on Foreign Corn.

Now we will Have a Peep at the Farmer 62 years ago when i was a Farmer's Boy to Plough and Sow, to Reap and Mow. In fact Boys Did not Do that, but the Song says so.

The Farmer Held the Plough. The son Drove. The Daughter milked and assisted in the Dairy. Do they do that to-Day? [1904]. When you Live Past your means or income, how can you expect to thrive? You must not think you need not work—even if you are a Farmer. Sixty years ago the farmer wore a white smock, the labourer a brown one. I se the Farmer go to Church in that dress.

Corn was £5 Per Quarter, a Labourer's wages seven or eight shillings a week, though a Schepperd got eleven shillings for he had Greater Responsibility Resting on his Shoulders. Sometimes he was up all night looking after Lambs and Cattle, so he Commanded a Good Wage.

Corn being so Dear and wages so Low, you might say the Farmer was well off. What the Farmer gained on Corn he Lost on meat. Meat was 3d., 4d., 5d., or 6d per pound. You could have a Sheep's head and pluck the lot for a shilling. They was Called watch and seals. Two or three women would get one between them. With respect to a bit of meat, i never se any the First ten years of my Life, only on Sunday.

Why was the meat so Cheap and Bread so Dear? Because the People had no money to Buy. They was Compelled to Have Bread or Starve, as many Did. If my Father's wages Had been spent in Bread alone, we could not Have had a Belly Full for there were ten of us. You se, all this is Regulated by Supply and Demand. All would be well if the workmen Had a Better Wage and could Buy Meat, but he had no mony.

Joseph Arch came into North Lincolnshire forty years ago to try and Lift up the Labourer. He Formed a Union and they Began to get a Better wage. The Farmers' combined not to employ any man in the union and they Smashed it up. Arch told the Farmers: 'You are making a Rod for your own Back.' All the Best of our Labourers Crossed the Seas and are Sending us Corn Cheaper than our Farmers can grow it. The Farmer is a Jackall for the Landlord, and toDay—1904—they are like the

Publican and Support the very men who Have Crushed them. What killed the Farmer is what is killing Hundreds of men in Towns. [High] Rents.

Agriculture is the Root of every other Branch of industry. Soon we shall have branches and no Roots. But it only Sleeps, for soon we shall get the right men into Parliament and they will wake it up.

Now we have the Largest Factory in England shut up—for Game and Pleasure; millions of men Drove into the Large Towns by Low wages and run up Rents; and all because the Demand is greater than the supply. Our Streets are filled with Prostitutes and three men are Ready to Do one man's work.

There's not really too many Men, but they are in the wrong Places. Sometimes I go and Look at the Farm I first went to work on. It employed fifteen men, their wives and families in summer. Today I se one man—a Shepperd. If we could only get the People Back under Better Conditions, and if only we Produced what we Consumed. That would be an improvement.

Joseph Chamberlain says 'I will Rise the Price of food and raw materials and Rise your wages.'* I Have always Proved that just the Reverse happens. Since 1846 my Wages are gone up—and so has a four pound loaf which was 9d., then a shilling,—and

---

* This is exactly what James Hawker has written. He probably meant to write 'I will *lower* the price of food . . .'

before Joseph's War it was 3d. It's not what you earn in wages that matters, it's what it will buy when you've got it. If you Had a House Full of Gold and no Food, what then? But the men on Chamberlain's platform who are Backing him up, Patting him on the Back, whispering in his ear, only want to Tax the Peoples' food so they can get more Rent. Since 1846 i have been able to buy as much Food for six shillings as Cost my Father £1 -3s—all through Free Trade.

Now let me Prove it by considering the situation before the War—and we know who is Responsible for that. The man who wants to Tax your Food.

Take six shillings and Divide it into three Parts. Two shillings worth of Bread, two of Sugar and two of Plums or Currants. These are not isolated articles but what we can't Do Without. Take eight loaves, 12 Pd. sugar, 12 Plums or Currants—and there are your six bob's worth. But if you had bought the same quantity sixty years ago, eight loaves would have cost you eight shillings, 12 Pd. sugar 9s.,— and it Has been 10 d. a Lump. And 12 Pd. Currants were six shillings—at 6d per Pound. So Much for Free Trade.

There was more work then, but you could do Nothing [with what was earned?] when you Done it. Are you going to Let Joseph take you Back to that just to please a few Dukes and Lords?

This fight is got to be Fought sooner or Later. And now Let us Look at the General who wants to Lead the Army of workers in England. i Have Had my Eye on him ever Since He became a Public Man, and i once Heard Bradlaugh say 'He's the Coming Man.'

When he first appeared it was not Long before he won the Highest qualification a man can win— the Confidence of His Fellow men. He Promised three horses and a Cow, one man, one vote, old age Pensions, Disestablishment of the English Church, and, after the assassination of Burke and Cavendish, He told Parnell and Justin McCarthy [?] that if he could only be Chief Secretary for Ireland he would assist them in every Reform they needed, including Home Rule.

What is this man's attitude to Home Rule today? There is no Bigger Enemy. But if the irish was Deserving of Home Rule then, why not now? Gladstone found in this man what the working Class will Find. He is not to be Trusted. the Grand Old Man put John Morley as Chief Secretary, and that so done Joe. Then when Gladstone Recommended Lord Rosebery as Leader of the House, that Done it again. As soon as the Old Man Brought in his Home Rule Bill, Joe Turned Traitor. He wrecked Gladstone's Government. Whoever Lives to see it will find he wrecks the Tory Government. The very men who

are using Joe as a Tool [will see it]. He once Spoke
of them as a Class who neither Toil nor Spin.
Salisbury Called him Jack Cade.

But we Hold the Trump Card in our Hands.
Only we are to much Eaten up with Drink and
Gambling to Play it. Men—be ashamed of your-
selves.

Some men are now blaming machinery for their
troubles. I once Heard Charles Bradlaugh say:
'When men are wise, they will see that the more
machinery is introduced, the Better for them.'

You cannot place any Restriction on the inge-
nuity of man. If you Do, and try to Prevent these
[developments], what a mistake we should make.
The Benefits through Machinery are Greater than
its injuries. Suppose i Cary you Back to the old
Coaching Days—which I well Remember and often
wish i could Forget.

It took four Days to Travel from London to
Liverpool. Now they Do it in a few hours. i Have se
the Coaches snowed up for Days. What sort of a
mess should we be in to Day if we Had no Steam or
machinery? Yet some of you Speke of machinery
the Same as some men Did 60 years ago. They were
called Luddites. These men thought machinery
would injure them. Yet what about the Bike?
Or the Motor? These things Have Been the means

of Fetching millions out of the Pockets of those who would not Have Spent one Penny in the interests of the workman. All these things have found employment for millions of men. Read the account of Coventry, a Town that was once going to Decay. No Town in England is now more Prosperous.

Have you never had a Peep at the working Class Riding to work on machines that cost £12? And then people say we are no Better off than we was 60 years ago. The only Ride i Can Remember was to Push a Gate wide open and then step on and Bang against a Gate post. If you Had any Food inside of you, it would Shake it out.

It is often said the agricultural labourer seemed a Deal Happier 60 years ago that what they seem to Day. Well, we know there are many men Better off in Prison than what they are out. But they would Rather be out. The Labourer 60 years ago was merely a Serf. Some will say 'Ah, but they had a Fat Pig to kill at Christmas.'

Just so. i will Show you How they got it. The Farmer was more Humane, Kinder hearted, and He allowed Privileges the Farmer today Don't allow. The Farmer of to Day is on the make, Like any other Employer of Labour. He wants all out of the Land without Putting anything in. It is the same with all other Employers. Farmers are impoverishing the Land, [industrialists] the People.

[76]

Now i will Show how the Labourers got their Pig.
Then i will Show you How many men Fed them.
The Farmer would Let any man at the Latter end
of Summer Have a small Pig ranging from twenty
to thirty Shillings in value and let him pay it Back
at sixpence a week. But to feed this pig the labourer
took most of the Food from there Master. i Have se
in one Labourer's House in 1846 a Sack of Beans, a
Sack of Barley, a Sack of Wheat—all stolen from
the master. Keeping these men in Poverty made
them Thieves. Poverty is the Mother of invention.
Poverty made me Poach.

Now you may say 'Where was the Police?'

There was none in Daventry till we got the County
Franchise and Redistribution. Then there was two
Constables—John Watts, a shoemaker, and Richard
Coleman, a Baker. Sometimes i Have Run to Fetch
Shoemaker Watts.

'What's the matter, Jimmy?' he'd say. 'Did you
say there was a fight? Let 'em Fight. I can't come
till I've Finished these Boots.'

So you may guess it was Easy to Steal.

Where Did they Have Corn From to Feed their
Pigs? Before the days of the threshing machine,
four or six men would be in a Large Barn all
through the winter like the one in the Possession of
John Morley in Oadby. They would use Flails to
knock out the corn. After being there all winter, they

[77]

would Do about as much as a machine would Do in Half a Day. This is where the men had the Corn from.

In my early Days of Poaching, i Have se much of this. Then there was a chance, too, of gleaning Corn. A woman with a large Family would Pick enough Corn almost to Feed a Pig if Her Husband was not inclined to be a Thief.

But there are more Commercial Thieves today with Plenty than what there was 60 years ago with Poverty. If we Don't want the Ranks of the unemployed swelling, we working men can Prevent it, but 60 years ago we Had no Chance. Then we had no Vote, to Day we Have. But there are thousands of men who Don't seem to know its value. Men, if I was able to give you a Tip Respecting Horse Racing, How Eager you would be to Put all on. Now Let me give you a Political Tip. If every man who wants to Better is Position and at the same time Benefit me and every man who Toils, vote for the Labour Candidates—not only at the next General Election but Has Long as you Live.

For i will Predict that Labour will Rule the world one day. It is only a matter of time. Don't be on the Losing Side. The Election will be on us before we know where we are, and if very working man Does his Duty, we shall se such a Victory as no man Dreams off.

Passing events Prove this. Every week we are seeing a Turning of the Tide Politicily, but what has Brought this Change on the People is the same that made me Poach. Bad times make men. If you Have no other Reason not to vote Tory, this one is Sufficient. The Class tried to Prevent you from Having the vote. My Father never Had one. Don't Forget this.

Farmers and Publicans are almost Brothers—who have always supported the men or class who have nearly brought ruin, but they can't see it. I have already said a Little about the Farmer. Let me add one word Respecting the Publican. He comes in for a Fair Share of Abuse from the Temperance Party, but he always commands my Respect because He Has to Have an unimpeachable Character before he is permitted to sell. How Different with other Tradesmen. I want to be fair to every man. During my 70 years i Have met with no encouragement to enter any Pub from any of these men.

Sixty years ago he Brewed his own ale at sevenpence per gallon. The Brewer had two and sixpence per day. Malt and Hops—if you got full up with them—would not make you ill. Today—1905—the publican has to Purchase his ale at double the price. It is preserved with Chemicals and the Brewer gets thousands a year. It makes you ill—and fills the Lunatic asylums with men and women who are a total wreck. The Publican as Helped to Do this by Sending these Great Brewers to Parliament.

Under the Tied House system, they have Robbed the Publican of his Liberty and Robbed the Public of Pure Beer. If I go into a Pub the worse for Drink, this man can't Refuse to Serve me, because if he don't sell much, he has to clear out. How are we to deal with the Drink question? No statesman can deal with it. The People must tackle it themselves. We must find some greater attraction than Pubs. Homes must be made more attractive and millions must be brought back to the Land. The interest in Drink is so deeply rooted in every Section of Society that it is dangerous to Meddle with it in Parliament.

Osborne Morgan has said I have asked for a Veto Bill. But it will be years before the Liberal Party attain power again.

We have six pubs in Oadby. Suppose we had closed three of them, would it have done any Good? The moment you have done that, you have not only robbed Peter to pay Paul but you will simply make the other pubs more attractive. Do you think that if there was no Hares at the Top of the village and plenty at the Bottom, I should not go after them? We could only solve the Drink problem by closing all the pubs and that we shall never Do. Let it alone.

X

PORTRAIT OF OADBY

I said that when I first came to Oadby the more I knew of it the better I liked it. I will have a few words of men who have gone and some still living.

I will first confess I was silly enough to take upon myself a Great Responsibility—a wife. Many men shirk this. I was in no hurry. It is said marry in haste and repent at Leisure, so I took my time. Then after being in Oadby but a few weeks I found the young woman I saw against the Wesleyan Chapel—and I have never regretted the day we met. I am not going to praise her. A Good Article needs no praise.

When I got wed I wanted to keep it a secret from all I could. The Militia was out at the time and her Brother George was in it. I asked leave on Sunday morning. Then him and myself walked from Dover Street to St. John's Church, met the Bride and Bridesmaid outside and found people two deep inside the church. After going through the ceremony the Minister—Mr. Barber—says to My Wife: 'You are Highly Honoured, being married in Scarlet.'

When we got outside Mrs. Chamberlain from Sopwith stood there. 'Ah, Collis,' she said, 'You've done it at last.'

It was not long before all Oadby knew. When we got back into Dover Street, Thomas Normans, Her eldest Brother, and I stood at threepence. As soon as it was opening time we had a pint of ale. Then I stood with a Brand New Wife and an Empty Pocket. I would rather start so than begin High and Come Down.

At the Bottom of the village near the childrens' playground Stood mud Houses fifty years ago. John Cartwright lived in the last that stood there. In those houses lived many men I knew, one of them a noted character called Cockey Robinson who once played the part of a Bear. He was at the end of a rope handled by a man of the name of Ludlam, commonly called Buck, and father to the present Buck who is still Living—1905. He carried a long pole and at intervals would poke the Bear in the Ribs, at the same time shouting. The street was soon Filled with a Delighted Throng. Candles was given to the Bear, then cabbagés were brought. Before he could fill his belly, Mrs. Robinson appeared and after giving the Bear a sound thrashing, broke up the entertainment.

Mr. John Gilbert, commonly called Tower, was another character. He was tall—six feet—clean shaven, courteous and fearless. He was never afraid to speak his mind. I have known him to walk into the Church in the middle of a Service, sit there for ten minutes and then take up his hat and walk out. He was a Sound Radical and the whole of his family take after him.

Then there was Hary Crib, George Pick, Charley Chucky Harris, John Roper, and Marriott, poor woman, who lay on a Bed of Affliction for years. She was a great sufferer and passed away a few months ago.

I knew Edward Sturges, a Farmer of Sheppard Hill. Teddy was a Poacher. Then there was William Chaundler, Joe Colver who Loved a Pint, a Pipe and a Dog; Thomas Sidans, [Siddons?], Jessie Levis and Mr. Graunt—all in Malting Lane, in a Square where Mrs. Ward's new Houses Stand. There Lived Mr. Colver Langham, Meakin and his Brother, Tom Parry, Tom Granger and others. There was Bob

Markham's Farther in Malling Lane, old Jim Ball and other Notables, all passed away. Harry Hill kept the Pub Called the Wheel—a very Funny Man. A man once went in and called for a Pint of ale. Harry Drank out of it without Being asked. The man complained. So Harry put the man on the Fire.

A few doors above lived John Weston—Nobber— a very powerful man, like me very fond of killing Game. i Have spent much time with this man, one of the Gamest men i Have ever met and one of the Tenderest Hearted. I was pleased to go with him because always you might be sure of coming Back. He was with me when i Shot the Hare that Caused me to Fly rather than Pay eight Pounds. Peraphs it may interest you to Look at this man in this Social Drama. After Shooting the Hare i Put it in a small Basket carried by John Norman, or Pink, as we called him. On our way Home we met Cook, the Head Keeper, and Ward the under-keeper. Ward wanted to Search the Basket. I got between Pink and Ward to Prevent that and he Struck me across my Back. I Collared him, put my Foot Behind His and Threw Him Heavily and then Knelt on him. I continued to Kneel on him while Pink got away with the Hare.

Cook said He'd Knock my Brains out if I didn't let him get up. Poor old Nobber. I threw this man Back, as Cook was saying 'If you Strike him, you won't Strike another. Let Him get up.'

Pink was then 300 yards away. Cook says to Ward 'Take off your coat and go after him.' After He Had run 50 yards, I had taken off my Coat. And before he had got 200 yards i Had Downed him again till Pink got Clean away.

These had £2 each to Pay and i Had £3 plus £5 revenue for Killing without a Licence. They would not have know I Had killed the Hare, but Pink threw it away and they found it.

A Little Higher up in the village lived Thomas Chamberlain, Franc smith where Mrs. Strang's Property Stands. A very powerful man, he once Picked me up and Held me at arm's length. He Has a son Thomas still Living. Then there was old Doctor Beasly and Doctor Jackson, George Allen, old Bill Weston, Mrs. Holyoake who's Father was very fond of a gun. There was J. Summerland in the Club yard, and a few good old Reformers—John Kirk, J. Waite, Tom Elliott, Mrs. Thompson, J. Bromly Mutton, Dick Grewcock, Andrew Ross the Baker and old Granny Sturgess. She kept a Pub where the Club House is. She Bought James Colver, my Pal, a Banjo, with the Bones, for me to keep his company together. James Colver was a Lad that Could Do anything but work. He was not a Bad Judge [of character ?].*

A little Higher up still lived Mr. Pywell, old sir

*or music?

[85]

Gilbert and Tom Gilbert—Brothers, Jack Lord, Tom Brooks, Peter Howard,—Black Dog—Jim, his Son, and old Topper Lubman. Old John Mellows was very Fond of a Long Clay Pipe—a son of St. Crispin. Poor old Robert Hensman still Lives. He must be nearly a 100, a man I've always Respected. He has children to comfort him in his old age. I wish many would try to imitate him.

Others who come to mind include Mrs. Wall, Edward Gilbert, Edward Goddard, Poor old Clocker Gilbert who is still Living, Thomas Hurst, George Allin, Ben Allin, George Weston, Daniel Dice, Mrs. Bishop and Jim Wright with two Sticks.

Billy Watts is a man I can't miss without a kind word. I have enjoyed his company many times. I never knew him do a wilful injury to anybody. He was very near getting me in Prison once, but he had no Bad intention. Billy was one of the best romancers I ever Heard. If he Did not always speak the Truth, I should like to see the man who does. I enjoyed it more than if it had been true. When he was trying to amuse you, you had to be careful not to get too near him or you would feel his elbow in your ribs, as a Reminder.

Now Billy had a very Strong Rival in Oadby, a man who said he had Better cattle than Billy. This was Tom Witmore. Billy told me of this little incident so that I could judge for myself. He was going to Market Harborough with his mare and cart after a very Rough Night. When he got through Kibworth, the wind had blown ten yards of the Turnpike up. He gave the mare her head, just spoke to Her and over they all went. 'Do you think Whitmore could do that ?' asked Billy. No, Billy, I don't. Poor old Billy.

Young Ball, Chad Granger and others set some snares some 46 years ago and the keepers found them. It was very cold weather and the keepers sat on guard with a large dog. Watching and sitting so long they was stiff with cold. They could not run when the men went to take up the snares. So they sent the dog after them. Young Ball cut the Dog's throat and killed it and the men got away.

When the Keepers got down near the hall they met Granger. He got two months. They did not discover the others. Mrs. Watts met me the same morning near Poors Field when going a-milking. With no bad intention she say 'I know who killed the Dog. I met him—Jimmy Collis.'

If the Keepers had met me I might have had two months. But I knew nothing about it. I had been out all night trying to knock a Pheasant out of Bed.

No man in Oadby had been in at the death of more Game than John Chamberlain, but he said nothing about it. Deep waters run Still. He still lives in Blaby Union.

He was a Preacher. Ditto Teacher.

Old Joe Cartwright once sat on the Bough of a Tree and sawed if off. Down he came with it. He was a good Shot, very fond of game, but he detested me.

Mrs. Thomas Glover told me many a time where a Hare was sitting, so I might go and Kill. Once I se Ted Ward, the Keeper after me. I carried a Gun in one hand and two Hares in the other. He turned another road so that he might give evidence against me. But although heavily handicapped I got away unknown.

Lawyer Spooner was well known. He would place his walking stick on John Hodges's meat and order the length of it and then Forget to Pay.

I remember Charles Robinson and Sam Robinson, and John Smith who Kept the Fox and is now a Butcher, still Living. Mr. and Mrs. Bassett were two Good Souls in Hill's Yard. John Hill was a very hale man. Then there was old John Green and the Reverend Gregory at the vicarage.

Robert Simons Kept a Shop where the Baptist Chapel now stands. I will relate a little incident respecting Mrs. Simons. Nearly fifty years ago I was Sitting on that bit of Land called New Knighton, about fifty yards from the Boundry Stone. One evening at about 8.30 p.m., I was waiting with my Gun for a Hare to come and Feed in the vegetables. It was a Lovely still night and I could Hear the

Little Children playing in the streets of Oadby. The Ground was covered with Snow. After Sitting a Short time I Pressed the Trigger of my Gun. A Hare with four Broken Legs was Bouncing about, shedding its blood on the white Snow and shouting at the Top of its voice. 'Ant-ant-ant'. I had never Heard one make more noise.

After killing and Putting it in my Pocket, I came on to the Road where the Trams start. I sat on some railings and had a nice quiet smoke. Policemen, as I have said, have no power to interfere once you are on the main road.

Soon I heard footsteps on the hard frozen snow. Coming towards Oadby came Mrs. Simons. 'Is that You, Collis?' she said.

'Yes,' I answered.

'Did you Hear that Man shoot that Child? I could Hear the Poor Dear Cry when I was up against Allen's Gate. Where was it?'

'About fifty yards from where we are standing,' I said.

'Where is the poor Little Thing?'

'In my pocket,' I said, pulling out the Hare.

I don't know her feelings, but she looked like a cat what had Lost a Mouse. We walked home together and whenever I se Mrs. Simons, she always smiles.

A pretty young Woman was Living with Mrs. S. at the time—called Steller Ann. Today it is Mrs.

George Ross of Wigston. A Little Higher up was old Tom Smith, the Coal Dealer, where the Baths stand. Tommy Quince, his wife and Donky, old Frank Freeman and others.

It used to be said that the Large House where Mr. Prentice Died was haunted and many strange things have been seen there. I never se anything. I should love to se a Ghost in the spirit. I've se Plenty in the Flesh.

Poor old Wilkinson was a man I have Been with many times. A very stout man, he was, and son of St. Crispin. He was not the Best of Workmen, but he was a plain, strong hand. When he had his shoe on his lap, his fat belly would hide it. We shan't forget this man for his kind thought for the poor of Oadby at Christmas. Rest in Peace.

Mr. Carter and Thomas Butcher were two very quiet strait men. Thomas still lives in Leicester union. Old Thomas Goddard employed many men and very Pleasant he was. He always had a smile for any one and was always willing to toss every one in the room for a quart for the benefit of the company.

My wife's father was a small, good-looking man who tried his very Best to set his Daughter against me, because I was so Reckless. He was only playing the Part of the Father, but he afterwards said I was not so Bad as He expected I Should be. Some of the worst young men are Single. But they often prove to be the best when married. No one loved to kill game better than this man. But in the latter part of his life he turned very steady, attended a Place of Worship and I believe he Died Happy.

Charley Voss was a character. I once heard Mr. Britten say to Charles: 'You don't Buy much ale, but you help drink a good lot.' Poor Charley had not much money to spend, but his jokes where as dry as his Throat.

Joe Ludlam Still Lives, one of the most Funny men I have ever met. I se im a short time ago. 'Jimmy,' he says, ''ow are you going on?'

Then he told me a man had just called him a liar. 'I told him I had a pair of glasses on through which I could see a thousand miles.' He said that was not true. 'Yes it is,' I told him. 'I can see the moon and that's the truth.'

I said Oadby intellectually and politicaly takes the cake. I mean what I said. Where you find ignorance among the working men, you will find them inclining towards the Class. Where you find men who Toil, intelligent men, they incline towards trying to Better the condition of their fellows.

One of the clearest proofs of this is seen in the way the Class tried to Keep the People ignorant and would do even today if they could Rob us of this blessing. I remember before we got the Franchise

that Lord Randolf Churchill said in the House of
Commons that the Agricultural Labourer was too
ignorant to vote. Do you think he was in earnest
when he said that? They have Throve on Ignorance,
but they knew the Reverse.

If you don't believe that Oadby is Game—politically, ask Jesse Collins. Ask him what he thinks of
them. He had such an encouraging Reception. He
lost not only his Temper but his manners, for he was
called by one man a Dam Liar. Ask Sir Thomas
Wright what he thinks of Oadby men. When seeking
County Council honours, he stood on the steps of the
Corn Exchange, Leicester. 'The Oadby men Done
me,' he said.

And when at an Election, they could not win at
the Ballett Box, they brought a gang of Roughs to
give Oadby men a Sound Thrashing. Ask these
Roughs what they think of Oadby men.

I was very pleased when Sir Thomas Wright was
defeated. I will tell you why. It is said you should
not speak ill of the Dead. But if a dead man de-
serves praise, give it him; if he don't and you speak
nothing but the truth, let us hear what you have
got to say. Most newspapers have spoken of Sir
Thomas very highly, but I don't take my advice
from them. It's their trade. I speak from experience.

Sir Thomas was the son of a Shoe Maker. He lived
in Cow Lane, Northampton. He was so poor he got

his Son in a Blue Coat School. So he was better educated than he would have been had it fallen to his father to procure the means for schooling. After leaving school he got into a Lawyer's Back Office and soon showed he Had a Fair Share of ability. He had taken a prominent part in many Elections, first as a Radical, then as a liberal, and finally as a Tory or unionist.

When I was enfranchised, my first vote was given to Charles Bradlaugh. At that time the Non-Conformists was very Bitter against this man. They sent all over England to try to get a Good man to oppose him. The reply that came from many good men including Sir Charles Dilke was 'You have a good man; put him in.'

Sir Thomas said he would stand and fight if they would get him 2,000 signatures. They got him that number and he issued his address as an advanced Liberal. At one of his meetings we made it so hot for him and proved that most of the names was Procured from School Children. He was so ashamed he retired in favour of Bradlaugh. He Retired because he could not win. Sir Thomas played every card Political and at the Latter part of his Life he had not a Trump.

Ye shall know men by there works.

One of our temperance friends in Oadby would

sometimes speak very strongly against the working mens' Club. Sometimes he would travel a little too far. Then, the men in the Club did not like it. He was a public servant, a member of the School Board and his intentions were very good. But his mode of trying to make the men Better by drinking less was Bad. As I have said before, you cannot drive a man, you can only Lead him.

What would this man think if an attack had been made on him for being a total abstainer? It might have been said that he was worse than a moderate drinker for he had no control over himself or he would not have had to abstain.

They determined to get their own Back at the School Board Election. They drove this man out and put me in, a Duty I was unfit to Fulfil. This shows you what stuff Oadby men are made of. They won't be sat on.

Being on the School Board threw me into the camp of many of the Leading Gentlemen in the village. I believe their only complaint about me was that I was a poacher. I remained on the School Board for six years—simply Because I se no chance of getting off it. At the second election, there were two more candidates than what was required. To save the Expense of an Election, me and Mr. Matthews, an old and Dutiful servant, retired. He was a gentleman I hope everyone in Oadby respects.

It was reported to me after my election to the Board that a Gentleman said, 'Things have come to a nice pass if we have to have an old Poacher on the School Board.' I don't believe all I Hear and very little of what I see. There is so much Deception in the world. But if that remark was true, he ought to live through the times that made me poach. Those were the dark days of protection. This man is one of Joseph Chamberlain's Commission—Mr. Corah.

At the first Parish Election, I was one of the members. Afterwards Mr. Corah joined the council too. We became close friends. In fact we got so close that I was given permission to Roam over his Beautiful Grounds and shoot. I took part in all the rook shooting. But I have never Troubled this gentleman a deal. I went several times to look for a Hare but could never find one. I knew the hares paid him visits, but they did not stop on his grounds. That favour has never been withdrawn. If I liked, I could go over his Land today. But when you give a poacher permission to kill game you take the Sugar out of the ginger bread. You rob him of the pleasure it is to an expert poacher to steal a march not only on the game but on the men who claim it for their own. I have poached more for Revenge than Gain. Because the Class poached upon my liberty when I was not able to defend myself.

XI

THE VILLAGE CONCERT

One Dear Old Friend, the first man I ever spoke to in Oadby, and one I shall never Forget, was John Newnham who Lived Next Door. He was so courteous and quiet and would try to Please every one. He would sometimes, like other Men, enjoy himself, but I Have never se him out of Temper. He was a very Tall Man, with no flesh on his bones, and he looked as Hard as Nails. He was a Singer at the Church and out of Church he was a High Kicker. Very Few men was Better than him. I once se him knock a Pipe off the tall mantle shelf in the White Horse Tap Room.

He once said He would make me a Good Singer and he tried to Learn me Notes, but my Head was too Thick. I think Has he did that i Contained Singing material, but was unable to Cultivate it.

One day he suggested we got up an Entertainment. This is the Programme:

John Newnham,	High Kicker,
Joseph Ditto,	Singer,
Mrs. Holyoake,	Violen,
Thos. Ditto,	Acrobat,
Thos. Norman,	Violen,
James Colver,	Banjo,
Me, on the	Bones,
William Colver,	Stump Oration.

We wanted Johnny Matthews and Minnie but Failed to get them.

We hired a Room at the Pub on the Left Hand Side and charged threepence Admission. When the time arrived we was in the Best of Form and we all knew it would be a Great Success. Who knows, we thought, there might be a Great Future for some of us.

Colver made good use of his Spare time—he always had Plenty of that—and was almost Perfect on the Banjo. I was not amiss on the Bones.

But we had one Misfortune which alone Prevented many of the Spectators from saying 'This is the Best and Cheapest Entertainment we Have ever witnessed'. Everything went off Grand till we reached Thomas Holyoake, the acrobat. The

Niggers Where Really good and i can Hardly find words to Describe them. But then the Acrobat was Hanging from a Beam eight feet High by his Toes. He was Hanging so Long we thought he was merely Prolonging the Entertainment. But to our surprise, He was Black in the Face. He could neither get up nor Down. This Realy Brought Down the House. The Mob opened Their Mouths so wide you could almost see what they Had had for T. If John Newnham Had not Have Reached him Down, He would Have Hung there till now.

Out of all this Talented Lot, there are but three Remaining.

XII
IF THEY ONLY KNEW

Swimming baths, a recreation ground and other things have been presented to the villagers of Oadby in recent years by one of the noblest of women. When she is laid in the Grave, you will be unable to find a Stone Large enough on which to write Her record of usefulness. Lady Rachel Ellis is her name. This woman will Die, but her Name will live, to be loved by millions yet unborn.

For more than forty years I had never heard this lady's voice till she came to open the Baths. I had heard it once before when she was a Little Child.

Strange to say, it was in reference to myself that she spoke. If she were to speak these mere five words today, I would accept them as a very Great Compliment. But forty-six years ago I accepted them just the reverse.

I will explain what happened. I shot a Hare and wounded it. It ran into Mr. Hutchinson's plantation. Mr. H. was this lady's father. I knew the hare would die, so I hid my gun and went to look for it, creeping about on my hands and knees.

Soon two children playing on the Lawn, both of very tender years, se me. 'Willie, Willie,' she cried to her brother. 'There's a man.'

Then away they flew.

I have many times wished that remark was true. I have tried to be one. But none of us is perfect.

Now I will return the compliment to the little girl on the lawn—Lady Rachel Ellis. It has taken me a long time to do it. Now I will pay it in the same number of words that she used. She is a Noble Woman. (Excuse that term Please).

It is said that every man has one chance in his life. I was selected caretaker of the Baths. My wife was taken ill—and has been ill from that Day to this with chest affection. I was compelled then to give up the Baths.

I have now given you a Rough Sketch of my

Rough Life. I will now comment a little on what I have laid before you. Meantime I must point out that when I said I did little poaching, don't think I did not kill any more. On my oath I will—if I am able—kill till I die.

When I came to Leicester fifty years ago, I went to work for Carlings, High Street. i Closed him a Pair of Mens' Bals Japs at 3/6. Today they are Done a deal better with machinery for fivepence. More money can be earned now too, and it can be earned more easily. Although I am now 70 years of age, I can earn more money now than I could at eighteen. We should be faring better if we had free trade. We might be Better Still if men done what Bradlaugh said.

I sometimes attended the meetings for the unemployed on market square, Leicester. I do not fall in with all I se and Hear there, but the speakers are men of very good intentions. But some of the men addressed had no right to move with Honest, Hardworking men. If there was anything to be got, they always got it. These men never did and never will find work. But bad times are their Harvest. I have se the Good Honest Workmen share with the worst out of charity—for the class I have described are always the fairest. When the unemployed marched through Oadby I se many of this type. As they came by I stood in the street with a Leicester friend. One of the unemployed came to my friend: 'How have you been getting on?' we asked.

'Bloody fine,' he answered, 'only we've not had quite enough booze. But we had our share.'

I asked my friend what the man was by trade. 'He's never done no work in his life,' he said. 'He's what we call "a corner boy".'

One Monday I heard a Friend from London advising these men. 'If you can't get food, go and take it from the Shopkeepers,' he shouted.

That was very bad advice for starving men. How easy a spark may kindle a flame. If you accept that advise, where are you going to begin? I know where you are going to end. In the workhouse infirmary.

I saw the shops Locked in 1845; I don't want to see that today—for the greatest sufferers are the little shopkeepers who are sometimes as Hard up as ourselves. It's not all Gold that Glitters. But most of the speechmaking was moderate considering the circumstances. The advise to take what you had not got might have been all right sixty years ago for then we had no way of bettering our condition. Today, we have the vote. I hope that at the General Election which is close upon us, every man will do his Duty.

One of the unemployed asked me one morning:

'Jim, if I can buy a four pound loaf for threepence and I haven't got the threepence, what use is free trade to me?'

'You've had your chances,' I told him. 'You might have quids in your pocket now. I knew you when you were drawing two pounds, five shillings each week and I was drawing half as much. I have never been without threepence since I began work.

'A man without money is a Fool. And many are bigger Fools with it. But are you going to condemn free trade because you have had opportunities and wasted them?'

I asked him if it was not easier to get threepence —if you had no money—than to get the shilling which we had to get sixty years ago?

'If you Se Life as I do,' I told him, 'you will see that our Creator never intended us to work like niggers. He pushes everything he can in our way for our benefit and hundreds and thousands of men won't accept it. Let them starve. But all working men are not fools. The working class of England today are worth millions. If we only knew, we might use the words Kruger used. It would stagger humanity. 'God bless the Working Class. They're worth more than four hundred millions.'

XIII

EVERY MAN A POACHER

I want to prove that all sections of Society poach. Magistrates, policeman, keepers, farmers if they get the chance. It's in our nature as Englishmen. A love for animal destruction has always been with us. If you never kill with your gun, net or Stone, how you love to se others do so.

Captain Stopford, the Magistrate of Daventry, said when I flew from home to escape a charge of Night Poaching: 'If we can only get hold of James, I'll make an Example of him.' This man a few years before was out Shooting partridges on the first of

September. Pheasants are not shot until a month later. I was watching him—and I'll tell you what for. If a wounded Hare came near me, I would help the Hare to get away from him. I see him put up a Covey of Pheasants. He let two Barrells at them and brought down five or six. A Lad He had with him was picking them up. When I see this I come out of my Hiding so that he might know that I knew what He Had Done. When any one does what they ought not to do, they generally Look Round to se if any one sees them and he se me. I had taken off my coat, pretending I was at work. He sent his Lad with Half a crown with the remark, 'Pa thought those were partridges. He says he hopes you won't mention it. You won't, will you, please? You are to take this and get a Drink.' i went and Bought some Ammunition and used it on this Man's Land. So you se it is in our Nature to Cop what We Can.

Now let me show you the difference between a Gentleman Poacher and a Gentleman Sportsman. If a Gentleman went out for sport, he would not bring down more than one with each shot. If he did, he would be robbing himself. If you had a farm, you might have four coveys of partridges averaging twelve in each covey a total of forty eight. Bring down only one at a time, and you'll have more sport.

I have seen Gentlemen when birds got up, refuse to shoot and put down their guns if no bird was right or left. These men are sportsmen. But Captain Stopford was like me—a poacher. He wanted all he could get. Next time I go to Daventry—if in the summer time—I will place a Dog Rose on his grave. No worse Dog ever lived. I should be ashamed to describe his moral character.

As I began with Fish poaching, let me Finish with this Sport. In Daventry there are two large Reservoirs containing very Large fish—Pike, Carp, Roach, Perch, Tench. I have never caught any other sort.

One reservoir is the property of Edward Burton, the other of Major Clarke. I have never known either of these Gentlemen to summons a man in my time although many men trespassed there in search of fish. But you don't find men today like some sixty years ago. Major Clarke kept a Coachman of the name of Jim Kent. He was a big, powerful man and played the part of Keeper. He had Rabbetts and Pheasants but I never saw Hares there although since leaving home, I have been there many times. I usually went at night—when living in Northampton—and used the Long Net with others. We carried many a Bag of Rabbetts away. We would take them to Weedon and then walk about five miles, sell our stuff at Buckley Warf to a man who would retail

them, and then come back home again with sometimes the best part of a quid each.

Sometimes we made more than this, sometimes
nothing. If the weather proved Bad we had our
Journey for nothing. You may wonder how we
captured the Fish. First we would go to the Canal
and catch small Bait and set Dead Lines for Pike.
Put twenty or thirty in and you would not have to
wait long before you had one. The Keeper would
set a net called Tramel at a certain time of the year
when the Pike were on the Run. I hardly knew what
the term meant, but this net would be set about
fifty yards from the Tale End or Shallow Part about
twelve foot deep, and among the weeds. This net
might be twenty yards in Length and was twelve
Feet deep, held up by large flat corks. When fish
were in these corks would move.

How did we get the fish out? Well, where there's
a will, there's a way. To swim to the net would be
dangerous because of the weeds—and I have seen
several drown in Daventry Reservoir through swimming in weeds—especially when they were out of
sight. If ever you get among weeds, turn at once on
your Back and float over them. Don't forget this.
You may get into strange water and find weeds just
when you think all is safe.

We bought a Ball of String at sixpence, tied a
Stone on the End and also a Pot Hook and threw it

over the net and pulled it out. Once in this way we brought in three Large Gold coloured Tench and several Pike. To get the net in again, thread the line through Double, pull it in and draw the line out and no one will be any the wiser.

How did the net kill or catch the fish? I should like you to know all about it for it might prove useful to you someday. One day when you have a lot of Spare Time and a Spare Bob or two, instead of going and Sitting in a Pub and Drinking—what Robs you of manliness—go and buy some thing and make a net as I have done; then when bad times come use it against the Class that caused the Bad Times.

These nets are called Single Walling and Double Walling. If the net was twelve feet deep, that portion that kills in twenty feet, you should do well. If you had Double Walling, you would have another net in larger mesh. When the fish are dashing about amongst the weeds, they go through the Large Mesh, strike the small, and then tumble through the large to lie helpless. It does not matter which side they strike if there is Double Walling, but if there is only single walling, they would only be caught one way. It is going through the Large mesh into the Small that does them. Then they hang down Helpless.

XIV

FOXES, FERRETTS AND
COURTING COUPLES

If I Had been Born an idiot and unfit to carry a gun—though with Plenty of Cash—they would have called me a Grand Sportsman. Being Born Poor, I am called a Poacher.

Now I think I have mentioned most of the men I knew when advanced in years and I have not spoken unkindly of any of them. The only people that I have Reason to speak Disrespectful of are Father and

Son. I am sorry to do this for if a man wants to rise in the Estimation of his fellow men, don't do it, I tell him, by Lowering others. Nothing gives me more pleasure than to Speak kindly of my Fellow men.

Mr. William Norman knew I had got one of the Best Ferretts a man could have. I had trained it to do anything. He was a very powerful Creature with only one eye. Yet if a Rabbitt would not Bolt he would pull him out Backwards out of a Drain. He once pulled out nine rabbits close to Streeten Hall. I lent the Ferrett to Mr. Norman while I went out in the Militia—and I never se it again. He told me any Lie he could think of. His Son, Jim, who still lives with one Leg in the Grave and one Not Far Off, once came to me while I sat at work asking if I would bring my gun and shoot a Hare he had found. I left my work, walked above a mile, Run the risk of being Done in, Shot the Hare, and then he put it in his pocket. I never received a penny from that day. Bad Luck to Jim and I hope Billy— his father—is not where I have been many times— out in the cold.

We had a man—Peter Taylor—who represented Leicester in Parliament from 1862–1881. He brought in Bills for the Abolition of the Game Laws year after year. But today I can't hear even a Labour

Candidate open his mouth on behalf of the countryman and game. So I se no way only to Kill All I Can.

There are very few men who have killed more
Foxes than me. Sitting so quietly so many times, I
have had so many chances. Not many poachers will
do this for they're not worth the Powder and Shot.
But if there was only one Fox left on Earth and I
could kill it, I would do. Though if the Class was as
fair to me as I would be to them, I would spare the
Fox.

There's only one I have spared. That was a few
years ago. I saw one sitting in the Top of a Willow
Tree. The trunk was Hollow, and He went up inside,
Crept through a Hole at the Top and then he lay
all winter. Now I will tell you why I spared him. It
was only half a mile from Stretton Gorse and if the
Hounds drew a blank at any time, I would tell the
Huntsman—for ten bob—that I would take him to
where he Lay. I know I should have got it. When I
first came to Oadby, to Encourage the men to preserve the Fox, the Hunstman or Master would give
one pound to the person reporting it. This money
was spent on drink. Today they still give ten shillings at odd times.

One word about the Polecat. Many people are
under the impression that this animal is a species

of the House Cat. I have asked many men if they have ever se one. They generally say yes. But when I ask them to Describe it, they can't. I have seen but one alive, and two stuffed.

When seven years of age I used to take a Labourer's Dinner—he lived next door—to the Farm I first went to work on. While the old man sat having his Dinner, a Dog he had with him began to scratch at a hole in some standing beans. 'Boy,' cried the labourer, 'go an Find a Bolt hole and Stop it up if you can. He's got a Rat.' I found the Bolt Hole. But instead of stopping it up I began to Dig it out with a Piece of Stick and in a few minutes the Dog had him. The old man say, 'Why boy, its a Pole cat.' Now after sixty-three years I can smell it. You have heard the remark, 'You stink like a Pole Cat.' There is a good reason for it.

I have seen Ferretts as large but the polecat is larger, more like a Badger. The Head is like a Ferrett's but more round. If you was to cut about eight inches of an inner Tube when blown up and stick a head and tail on to it, that would be about the shape of the polecat. I don't think you would ever find one today though there is a Stuffed one in a Glass Case inside a Pub kept by Henry White in Infirmary Square, Leicester.

I have spent hours in that lane sitting like a cat.

The more quiet you sit, the better chance of getting Game. My biggest Enemies—Keepers and Police—don't really worry a poacher so much as Courting Couples. They generally get into a nice corner or nook where they think they are out of all Danger of being Heard. But they forget that a Poacher may be near. If you only knew what I have Heard in the Lanes, you would laugh. I have heard Promises made, but not kept. Half way down one lane used to be a Bank close to the Dyke. Here I would hide, laying my Gun on the bank, and wait till a Rabbitt, Hare or Pheasant made its appearance.

One evening at 6.30 p.m.—for I looked at my watch—a young couple came and sat on this Bank in Front of me. I was in hopes it would only be for a few minutes, but there they sat and I dare not come out. I would have been too ashamed. They would have thought I had got there on purpose. So there I sat, cramped up and not daring to move for an hour and a half. Rather than face such an adventure again, I would rather be cremated alive. But what I heard then, not a soul has ever known but I have kept my Eye on them to see if he or she had kept their Promises. They duly wed and appear very Happy; a Little Family are springing up.

Try to imitate the Timid Hare and get out into the open when you have a Little Secret to tell. Do not sit where there are Preserved Game or you may Sit Close to a Poacher.

I was sitting in Gorse Lane one morning some ten years ago before it was light. I was waiting for anything with my Gun. Two Policemen, a Farmer and Keeper came by me at Peep of Day, carrying Long Nets and Rabitts. They had been out most of the night. They are all Living. One Policeman has been made a Sergeant, the other an Inspector, and the Farmer is Driving a Tramcar. This only shows you what Life is.

THE END

James Hawker's Journal

A Victorian Poacher

EDITED AND INTRODUCED
BY
GARTH CHRISTIAN

ILLUSTRATED BY
LYNTON LAMB

OXFORD LONDON NEW YORK

OXFORD UNIVERSITY PRESS

1978

Oxford University Press, Walton Street, Oxford OX2 6DP

OXFORD LONDON GLASGOW
NEW YORK TORONTO MELBOURNE WELLINGTON
KUALA LUMPUR SINGAPORE JAKARTA HONG KONG TOKYO
DELHI BOMBAY CALCUTTA MADRAS KARACHI
IBADAN NAIROBI DAR ES SALAAM CAPE TOWN

ISBN 0 19 281255 6

© Oxford University Press 1961

First published 1961
Reprinted 1962
First issued as an Oxford Paperback 1978

Printed in Great Britain by
J. W. Arrowsmith Ltd., Bristol